VIRGO
2000

D0676232

With love to Bill, Jean, Rob and Shani

This is the third year that I've written these books and it's about time I thanked all the people who help me to put them together. I have worked with some of them since the beginning of the books, and others have only recently started lending me their help, but I am immensely grateful to them all. So thank you, Nova Jayne Heath, Nicola Chalton, Nick Robinson and everyone else at Robinson Publishing for being such a great team to work with. Thanks to Chelsey Fox for all her agenting skills. And a huge thank you to Annie Lionnet and Jamie Macphail for their tireless work.

VIRGO
2000

Jane Struthers

First published in 1999 by Parragon

Parragon
Queen Street House
4 Queen Street
Bath BA1 1HE
UK

Produced by Magpie Books, an imprint of
Robinson Publishing Ltd, London

Illustrations courtesy of Slatter-Anderson, London

ISBN 0 75252 895 5

A copy of the British Library Cataloguing-in-Publication Data
is available from the British Library

Printed and bound in the EC

CONTENTS

Dates for 2000

Virgo 22 August – 21 September

Libra 22 September – 22 October

Scorpio 23 October – 21 November

Sagittarius 22 November – 20 December

Capricorn 21 December – 19 January

Aquarius 20 January – 18 February

Pisces 19 February – 19 March

Aries 20 March – 18 April

Taurus 19 April – 19 May

Gemini 20 May – 20 June

Cancer 21 June – 21 July

Leo 22 July – 21 August

YOUR VIRGO SUN SIGN

This chapter is all about your Sun sign. I'm going to describe your general personality, as well as the way you react in relationships, how you handle money, what your health is like and which careers suit you. But before I do all that, I want to explain what a Sun sign is. It's the sign that the Sun occupied at the time of your birth. Every year, the Sun moves through the sky, spending an average of 30 days in each of the signs. You're a Virgo, which means that you were born when the Sun was moving through the sign of Virgo. It's the same as saying that Virgo is your star sign, but astrologers prefer to use the term 'Sun sign' because it's more accurate.

 **Character**

Some signs always get a good press, but Virgo always seems to attract a heap of criticism. 'Oh, you're a *Virgo*!' people say to you as if that explains everything, and you just know they're running through a checklist of horror traits in their head. For instance, you may think that you're a perfectionist but they'll call it fussing about tiny details. And you'll believe that you're modest but they'll dismissively say that you lack confidence.

Of course, there's an element of truth in all this, but the story isn't quite that simple. Because you belong to the Earth element, you take a very practical approach to life. That makes you wonderfully methodical and sensible, and also means that you're a tower of strength in a crisis. People rely on you but they may also take you for granted. Yes, you can occasionally go over the top and worry about the smallest little thing, but usually you're able to maintain a balance and keep matters in proportion.

Yes, you're certainly modest, and you hate to put yourself forward. When people compliment you (and you can't pretend that they don't, even if you do tend to shrug off their comments), you often blush, feel uncomfortable or ignore the remark completely. Even if half of you feels pleased, the other half is reminding yourself that you could have done everything so much better.

Relationships

One of the biggest problems stems from your reluctance to show your true feelings. Somehow you find it embarrassing and difficult to let people know how you feel, perhaps because it reveals the vulnerable side of your personality that you're always at pains to cover up. This can cause misunderstandings with loved ones, especially when you're under pressure. This is when your most unattractive trait comes to the surface: your ability to carp and criticize. There are times when your standards are so high that no one can ever hope to live up to them, and you'll waste no time in telling them so. You've no doubt heard a lot about this over the years from people who've been on the receiving end of your sharp comments, and who are still wincing. You need to learn to relax more, to think before you speak and to let your natural kindness come to the fore.

What people may not realize is that, for all the harsh things you can say to them, the internal dialogue you have with yourself is a lot worse. You may criticize other people but you're a lot harder on yourself. 'Could do better' just about sums it up. You really put yourself through the mill.

Money

This is one of the areas where you really come into your own, because the combination of your Earth element and your intelligent ruler, Mercury, makes you a formidable number-cruncher. You like to keep track of where you stand financially, and even if that doesn't happen in reality you'll keep promising yourself that you're going to pull your socks up.

It's not that you're miserly, but you don't like wasting money. You need to know that every penny you spend has been accounted for. You've got a good eye for a bargain and don't feel happy about splashing out on frivolous luxuries or little treats you rarely believe that you deserve such fripperies.

When you need to spend money on anything important or expensive, you'll spend a lot of time weighing up the pros and cons beforehand. You'll probably also do a lot of research to make sure you buy the right model and will question the salesperson at length – woe betide them if they don't have all the answers!

If you want to invest some money, you'll be happiest if you can seek sound financial advice first. You're reluctant to take any kind of risk, so will prefer to know that your capital is growing steadily rather than in volatile fits and starts.

Health

Every sign has a favourite hobby, and health is a big preoccupation for many Virgos. At best, you're very interested in staying healthy and are always keen to ensure you're eating the best possible diet and are getting plenty of exercise. You treat your body like a sophisticated machine that needs a lot of care and maintenance. At worst, you're a bit of a hypochondriac whose favourite bedtime reading is a medical encyclopedia – then you can lie awake all night worrying about all the ailments you've so obviously suffering from.

Stress and anxiety are definitely among your biggest health challenges. If there were Olympic gold medals for worrying, your mantelpiece would be groaning under the weight of them all. Once you start to fret, your digestive system (which is vulnerable and sensitive at the best of times) begins to get snarled up, with stomach upsets, constipation and irritable bowels. Stress can also play havoc with your health, so it's important for you to work it off with plenty of exercise and fresh air. And you must learn to relax!

It's very important for you to eat food that suits your metabolism, and many Virgos benefit from a wholefood, organic or vegetarian diet. Not only does this help your digestion to work better, it also makes you feel much more energetic and less tired.

Career

The rest of the world relies on Virgos. You're so organized and practical that you excel at making sure offices, businesses and organizations run smoothly. Without you, things tend to grind to a halt because no one else knows what's going on or how things work. If you're a typical Virgo, you'd rather take a back seat than be in the front line. You feel uncomfortable if you have to spend too long in the spotlight, but you thrive on being a valued member of a support team or advisory committee. In fact, any way in which you can be of service will show you at your best. You should give yourself a well-deserved pat on the back!

Among the professions that are right up your street are being an agent, secretary, teacher, writer, critic, scientist, doctor or nurse. You have a very enquiring mind, so need a job that stretches your brain and lets you make the most of your considerable intellect. You'll hate any job that bores or stultifies you, or which doesn't make the most of your tremendous potential. Give yourself a vote of confidence, Virgo – after all, the rest of us did, long ago!

MERCURY AND YOUR COMMUNICATIONS

Where would we be without Mercury? This tiny planet rules everything connected with our communications, from the way we speak to the way we get about. The position of Mercury in your birth chart describes how fast or how slow you absorb information, the sorts of things you talk about, the way you communicate with other people and how much nervous energy you have.

Mercury is an important part of everyone's birth chart, but it has extra meaning for Geminis and Virgos because both these signs are ruled by Mercury.

Mercury is the closest planet to the Sun in the solar system, and its orbit lies between the Earth and the Sun. In fact, it is never more than 28 degrees away from the Sun. Mercury is one of the smallest known planets in the solar system, but it makes up in speed what it lacks in size. It whizzes around the Sun at about 108,000 miles an hour, to avoid being sucked into the Sun's fiery mass.

If you've always wondered how astrology works, here's a brief explanation. Your horoscope (a map of the planets' positions at the time of your birth) is divided up into twelve sections, known as 'houses'. Each one represents a different area of your life, and together they cover every aspect of our experiences on Earth. As Mercury moves around the heavens each year it progresses through each house in turn, affecting a particular part of your life, such as your health or career. If you plot its progress through your own chart, you'll be able to make the most of Mercury's influence in 2000. That way, you'll know when it's best to make contact with others and when it's wisest to keep your thoughts to yourself.

Mercury takes just over one year to complete its orbit of the Earth, but during this time it doesn't always travel forwards, it also appears to go backwards. When this happens, it means that, from our vantage point on Earth, Mercury has slowed down to such an extent that it seems to be backtracking through the skies. We call this retrograde motion. When Mercury is travelling forwards, we call it direct motion.

All the planets, with the exception of the Sun and Moon, go retrograde at some point during their orbit of the Earth. A retrograde Mercury is very important because it means that during this time our communications can hit delays and snags. Messages may go missing, letters could get lost in the post, appliances and gadgets can go on the blink. You may also find it hard to make yourself understood. In 2000, there are several periods when Mercury goes retrograde. These are between 21 February and 14 March, 23 June and 17 July, and between 18 October and 8 November. These are all times to keep a close eye on your communications. You may also feel happiest if you can avoid signing important agreements or contracts during these times.

To plot the progress of Mercury, fill in the blank diagram on page 8, writing '1' in the section next to your Sun sign, then numbering consecutively in an anti-clockwise direction around the signs until you have completed them all. It will now be easy to chart Mercury's movements. When it is in the same sign as your Sun, Mercury is in your first house, when he moves into the next sign (assuming he's not going retrograde) he occupies your second house, and so on, until he reaches your twelfth house, at which point he will move back into your first house again.

Diagram 1

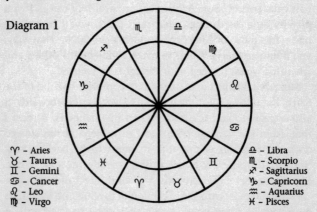

♈ – Aries
♉ – Taurus
♊ – Gemini
♋ – Cancer
♌ – Leo
♍ – Virgo

♎ – Libra
♏ – Scorpio
♐ – Sagittarius
♑ – Capricorn
♒ – Aquarius
♓ – Pisces

Here are the houses of the horoscope, numbered from one to twelve, for someone born with the Sun in Aquarius.

Diagram 2

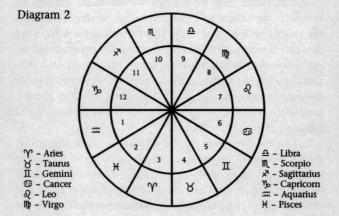

♈ – Aries
♉ – Taurus
♊ – Gemini
♋ – Cancer
♌ – Leo
♍ – Virgo

♎ – Libra
♏ – Scorpio
♐ – Sagittarius
♑ – Capricorn
♒ – Aquarius
♓ – Pisces

MERCURY'S ENTRY INTO THE SIGNS IN 2000
(All times are given in GMT, using the 24-hour clock)

January
Mercury is in Capricorn when 2000 begins

18	22:21	Aquarius

February

5	08:10	Pisces
21	12:47	Retrograde in Pisces

March

14	20:40	Direct in Pisces

April

13	00:18	Aries
30	03:54	Taurus

May

14	07:11	Gemini
30	04:28	Cancer

June

23	08:33	Retrograde in Cancer

July

17	13:21	Direct in Cancer

August

7	05:43	Leo
22	10:12	Virgo

September

7	21:23	Libra
28	13:29	Scorpio

October

18	13:42	Retrograde in Scorpio

November

7	07:29	Retrograde into Libra
8	02:29	Direct in Libra
8	21:43	Scorpio

December

3	20:27	Sagittarius
23	02:04	Capricorn

As 2000 begins, Mercury is moving through the final degrees of Capricorn, so it is in whichever house corresponds with the sign of Capricorn in your diagram. For instance, if you're an Aquarian, Mercury will move into your own sign at 22:21 GMT on 18 January and will occupy your first house. You can then read the explanation below telling you what to expect at this time. Mercury next moves signs at 08:10 GMT on 5 February, when he moves into Pisces. So if you're an Aquarian, Mercury will now be in your second house.

Mercury in the First House

This is a very busy time for you and you're completely wrapped up in your own ideas and concerns. Even if you aren't usually very chatty, you certainly are at the moment. However, you will much prefer talking about yourself to listening to other people! You've got lots of nervous energy at the moment and you'll enjoy getting out and about as much as possible. Look for ways of burning off excess energy, such as going for brisk walks or doing things that require initiative. This is a great opportunity to think about ways of pushing forward with ideas and getting new projects off the ground.

Mercury in the Second House

This is a great time to think about things that mean a lot to you. These might be beliefs, philosophies or anything else that gives meaning to your life. It's also a good time to consider the people that make your world go round. Do you devote enough time to them? You should also spare a thought for your finances, because this is a perfect opportunity to scrutinize them and make sure everything is in order. You could get in touch with someone who can give you some financial advice, or you might do some research into how to put your money to good use.

Mercury in the Third House

Chatty? You bet! This is probably when you're at your most talkative, and you'll enjoy nattering away about whatever pops into your head. You'll love talking to whoever happens to be around, but you'll get on especially well with neighbours, people you see in the course of your daily routine and close relatives. You'll soon start to feel restless if you have to spend too long in one place, so grab every opportunity to vary your schedule. You'll love taking off on day trips, going away for weekend breaks or simply abandoning your usual routine and doing something completely different. Communications will go well and you'll love playing with gadgets and appliances.

Mercury in the Fourth House

Your thoughts are never far away from your home and family life at the moment. You may be thinking about ways of improving your living standards and you could talk to people who can give you some advice. You're also wrapped up in thoughts of the past, and you may even be assailed by memories of far-off events or things you haven't thought about in ages. Pay attention to your dreams because they could give you some invaluable insights into the way you're feeling. Watch out for a slight tendency to be defensive or to imagine that people are trying to get at you. It's a lovely time for getting in touch with your nearest and dearest who live a long way away.

Mercury in the Fifth House

You'll really enjoy putting your mind to good use at the moment, especially if you do things that are based on fun. For instance, you might get engrossed in competitions, jigsaw puzzles, crosswords and quizzes, especially if there's the chance of winning a prize! Children and pets will be terrific company and you'll love romping with them. However, you may find that they're a lot more playful than usual. You may even be on the receiving end of some practical jokes. It's a super time to go on holiday, particularly if you're visiting somewhere you've never been before. Your social life promises to keep you busy and you'll find it easy to talk to loved ones about things that matter to you.

Mercury in the Sixth House

This is the ideal time of year to think about your health and well-being. Are you looking after yourself properly? If you've been battling with some strange symptoms, this is the perfect opportunity to get them investigated so you can put your mind at rest. You'll enjoy reading about medical matters, such as immersing yourself in a book that tells you how to keep fit or extolling the virtues of a specific eating plan. Your work might also keep you busy. Colleagues and customers will be chatty, and you could spend a lot of time dealing with paperwork or tapping away on the computer. It's a great time to look for a new job, especially if that means scanning the newspaper adverts, joining an employment agency or writing lots of application letters.

Mercury in the Seventh House

Communications play an important role in all your relationships at the moment. This is your chance to put across your point of view and to keep other people posted about what you think. You may enjoy having lots of chats with partners or you might have something important to discuss. Either way, the key to success is to keep talking! You're prepared to reach a compromise, so it's a marvellous time to get involved in negotiations and discussions. You'll also find that two heads are better than one right now, so it's the ideal time to do some teamwork. You'll enjoy bouncing your ideas off other people and listening to what they have to say.

Mercury in the Eighth House

It's time to turn your attention to your shared resources and official money matters. So if you share a bank account with your partner, you should check that everything is running smoothly. You might even decide to open a new account that suits you better or that pays a higher rate of interest. Speaking of accounts, this is an excellent time to fill in your tax return or complete your accounts for the year because you're in the right frame of mind for such things. This is also a good time to think about your close relationships. Do they bring you the emotional satisfaction that you need or is something missing? If you think there's room for improvement, talk to your partner about how to make things better between you.

Mercury in the Ninth House

The more you can expand your mental and physical horizons now, the happier you'll be. It's a time of year when you're filled with intellectual curiosity about the world and you long to cram your head with all sorts of facts and figures. You might decide to do some studying, whether you do it on a very informal basis or enrol for an evening class or college course. You'll certainly enjoy browsing around bookshops and library shelves, looking for books on your favourite subjects. Travel will appeal to you too, especially if you can visit somewhere exotic or a place that you've never been to before. You might become interested in a different religion from your own or you could be engrossed in something connected with philosophy, history or spirituality.

Mercury in the Tenth House

Spend some time thinking about your career prospects. Are you happy with the way things are going or does your professional life need a rethink? This is a great opportunity to talk to people who can give you some good advice. It's also an excellent time to share your ideas with your boss or a superior, especially if you're hoping to impress them. You could hear about a promotion or some improved job prospects, or you might decide to apply for a completely new job. It's also a marvellous opportunity to increase your qualifications, perhaps by training for something new or brushing up on an existing skill. You'll find it easier than usual to talk to older friends and relatives, especially if they can sometimes be a little tricky or hard to please.

Mercury in the Eleventh House

This is a great time to enjoy the company of friends and acquaintances. You'll love talking to them, especially if you can chat about subjects that make you think or that have humanitarian overtones. All sorts of intellectual activities will appeal to you at the moment. If your social circle is getting smaller and smaller, grab this chance to widen your horizons by meeting people who are on the same wavelength as you. For instance, you might decide to join a new club or society that caters for one of your interests. It's also a good opportunity to think about your hopes and wishes for the future. Are they going according to plan, or should you revise your strategy or even start again from scratch?

Mercury in the Twelfth House

You're entering a very reflective and reclusive period when you want to retreat from the madding crowd and have some time to yourself. You might enjoy taking the phone off the hook and curling up with a good book, or you could spend time studying subjects by yourself. There will be times when you feel quite tongue-tied, and you'll find it difficult to say exactly what you mean. You may even want to maintain a discreet silence on certain subjects, but make sure that other people don't take advantage of this by putting words into your mouth. You could be the recipient of someone's confidences, in which case you'll be a sympathetic listener. If you want to tell someone your secrets, choose your confidante wisely.

LOVE AND THE STARS

Love makes the world go round. When we know we're loved, we walk on air. We feel confident, happy and joyous. Without love, we feel miserable, lonely and as if life isn't worth living. If you're still looking for your perfect partner, this is the ideal guide for you. It will tell you which Sun signs you get on best with and which ones aren't such easy-going mates. By the way, there is hope for every astrological combination, and none are out and out disasters. It's simply that you'll find it easier to get on well with some signs than with others.

At the end of this section you'll see two compatibility charts – one showing how you get on in the love and sex stakes, and the other one telling you which signs make the best friends. These charts will instantly remind you which signs get on best and which struggle to keep the peace. Each combination has been given marks out of ten, with ten points being a fabulous pairing and one point being pretty grim. Find the woman's Sun sign along the top line of the chart, then look down the left-hand column for the man's sign. The square where these two lines meet will give you the result of this astrological combination. For instance, when assessing the love and sex compatibility of a Leo woman and a Cancerian man, they score six out of ten.

🧝 Virgo

As you might imagine, Virgos are happy with their fellow Earth signs of Taurus and Capricorn because they share the same practical attitude. A Virgo enjoys the steady, reassuring company of a Taurean, and they might even learn to relax a little instead of worrying themselves into the ground over the slightest problem. When two Virgos get together it can be too much of a good thing. Although at first they'll love talking to someone who shares so many of their preoccupations and ideas, they can soon drive one another round the bend. When a Virgo first meets a Capricorn they're delighted to know someone who's obviously got their head screwed on. It's only later on that they wish the Capricorn could lighten up every now and then.

Virgos get on well with Cancerians, Scorpios and Pisceans, the three Water signs. A Virgo enjoys being looked after by a considerate Cancerian, although they'll worry about their waistline and may get irritated by the Cancerian's super-sensitive feelings. You can expect plenty of long, analytical conversations when a Virgo gets together with a Scorpio. They both love getting to the bottom of subjects and will endlessly talk things through. They'll also get on extremely well in the bedroom. Pisces is Virgo's opposite sign, but although some opposites thrive in each other's company, that isn't always the case with this combination. The Virgo could soon grow impatient with the dreamy Piscean and will long to tell them a few home truths.

Although the other Earth signs don't usually get on well with Air signs, it's different for Virgos. They understand the intellectual energies of Geminis, Librans and Aquarians. A Virgo thrives in a Gemini's company, and they spend hours chatting over the phone if they can't get together in person. It's difficult for them to discuss their emotions, however, and they may never tell each other how they really feel. A Virgo admires a sophisticated, charming Libran, and marvels at their diplomacy. How do they do it? Expect a few sparks to fly when a Virgo pairs up with an Aquarian, because both of them have very strong opinions and aren't afraid to air them. The result is a lot of hot air and some vigorous arguments.

The three Fire signs – Aries, Leo and Sagittarius – are a source of endless fascination to a Virgo. They've got so much energy! A Virgo finds an Arien exciting but their relationship could be short-lived because the Virgo will be so irritated by the Arien's devil-may-care attitude to life. When a Virgo pairs up with a Leo, they'll be intrigued by this person's comparatively lavish lifestyle but their own modest temperament will be shocked if the Leo enjoys showing off. A Virgo is able to talk to a Sagittarius until the cows come home – they're both fascinated by ideas, although the precise Virgo will first be amused, and then irritated, by the Sagittarian's rather relaxed attitude to hard facts.

Libra

Of all the members of the zodiac, this is the one that finds it easiest to get on with the other signs. Librans get on particularly well with Geminis and Aquarians, their fellow Air signs. A Libran is enchanted by a Gemini's quick brain and ready wit, and they enjoy endless discussions on all sorts of subjects. When two Librans get together, they revel in the resulting harmonious atmosphere but it's almost impossible for them to reach any decisions – each one defers to the other while being unable to say what they really want. A Libran is intrigued by the independence and sharp mind of an Aquarian, but their feelings could be hurt by the Aquarian's emotional coolness.

Libra enjoys being with the three Fire signs – Aries, Leo and

Sagittarius. Libra, who often takes life at rather a slow pace, is energized by a lively Arien, and they complement one another's personalities well. However, the Libran may occasionally feel hurt by the Arien's single-mindedness and blunt speech. A Libran adores the luxury-loving ways of a Leo, and they'll both spend a fortune in the pursuit of happiness. They also get on well in the bedroom. When a Libran gets together with an exuberant Sagittarian, they'll have great fun. All the same, the Sagittarian need for honesty could fluster the Libran, who adopts a much more diplomatic approach to life.

Although the other two Air signs can find it hard to understand members of the Water element, it's different for Librans. They're more sympathetic to the emotional energies of Cancerians, Scorpios and Pisceans. A Libran delights in the protective care of a Cancerian, but those ever-changing Cancerians moods may be hard for a balanced Libran to take. Those deep Scorpio emotions will intrigue the Libran but they may quickly become bogged down by such an intense outlook on life and will be desperate for some light relief. As for Pisces, the Libran is charmed by the Piscean's delicate nature and creative gifts, but both signs hate facing up to unpleasant facts so this couple may never deal with any problems that lie between them.

Libra enjoys the reliable natures of Taurus, Virgo and Capricorn, the Earth signs. A Libran appreciates the company of a relaxed and easy-going Taurean, although they may sometimes regret the Taurean's lack of imagination. When a Libran and a Virgo get together, the Libran enjoys the Virgo's mental abilities but their critical comments will soon cut the Libran to the quick. The Libran may not come back for a second tongue-lashing. A Libran understands the ambitions of a Capricorn, and likes their steady nature and the way they support their family. However, there could soon be rows about money, with the Libran spending a lot more than the Capricorn thinks is necessary.

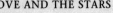

Scorpio

Not every sign gets on well with its fellow members, yet an astonishing number of Scorpios pair up. They feel safe together because they know the worst and best about each other. When things are good, they're brilliant but these two can also bring out the worst in each other, with intense silences and brooding sulks. A Scorpio enjoys the tender ministrations of a loving Cancerian, and adores being with someone who's so obviously concerned about their welfare. Feelings run deep when a Scorpio pairs up with a Piscean, although the Scorpio may become impatient with the Piscean's reluctance to face up to unpalatable truths.

The three Earth signs, Taurus, Virgo and Capricorn, are well-suited to the Scorpio temperament. Those astrological opposites, Scorpio and Taurus, enjoy a powerful relationship, much of which probably takes place in the bedroom, but whenever they have a disagreement there's an atmosphere you could cut with a knife, and neither of them will be prepared to admit they were in the wrong. A Scorpio is attracted to a neat, analytical Virgo but their feelings will be hurt by this sign's tendency to criticize. What's more, their pride stops them telling the Virgo how they feel. The Scorpio admires a practical Capricorn, especially if they've earned a lot of respect through their work, but this could be a rather chilly pairing because both signs find it difficult to show their feelings.

When you put a Scorpio together with one of the three Fire signs, they'll either get on famously or won't understand one another at all. A Scorpio revels in the lusty Arien's sex drive, although they'll soon feel tired if they try to keep up with the Arien's busy schedule. The combination of Scorpio and Leo packs quite a punch. They're both very strong personalities, but they boss one another around like mad and find it almost impossible to achieve a compromise if they fall out. A Scorpio likes to take life at a measured pace, so they're bemused by a Sagittarian's need to keep busy all the time. In the end, they'll become fed up with never seeing the Sagittarian, or playing second fiddle to all their other interests.

Scorpio is bemused by the three Air signs – Gemini, Libran and Aquarius – because they operate on such completely different wavelengths. A Scorpio can be good friends with a Gemini but they're at emotional cross-purposes, with the Scorpio's intense approach to life too much for a light-hearted Gemini to cope with. Emotions are also the bugbear between a Scorpio and a Libran. Everything is great at first, but the Scorpio's powerful feelings and dark moods will eventually send the Libran running in the opposite direction. You can expect some tense arguments when a Scorpio pairs up with an Aquarian – they're both convinced that they're right and the other one is wrong.

♐ Sagittarius

When a Sagittarian pairs up with a fellow Fire sign, there's plenty of warmth and the odd firework. A Sagittarian is thrilled by the adventurous spirit of an Arien, and they love exploring the world together. There are plenty of tall tales when a Sagittarian gets together with a Leo – they'll try to outdo each other, dropping names and recounting their great-est triumphs. If the Leo is slightly pompous, the Sagittarian is able to take them down a peg or two, but they must beware of hurting the Leo's feelings. As for two Sagittarians, they'll spur each other on and encourage one another to gain as much experience of life as possible. You probably won't be able to move in their house for books.

With their endless curiosity about the world, Sagittarians understand the intellectual Air signs very well. A Sagittarian enjoys the chatty company of a Gemini and, because they're opposite numbers in the zodiac, the Sagittarian is able to encourage the Gemini to see things through and explore them in more detail than usual. A refined and diplomatic Libran will try to teach the blunt Sagittarian not to say the first thing that pops into their head. However, the Sagittarian may eventually find the Libran's sense of balance rather trying – why can't they get more worked up about things? There's plenty of straight talking when a Sagittarian teams up with an Aquarian – they both have a high regard for honesty. The independent Sagittarian respects the Aquarian's need for freedom, but may feel rather stung by their periods of emotional coolness.

A Sagittarian will struggle to understand the Earth signs. They respect the Taurean's ability to work hard but they're driven to distraction by their reluctance to make changes and break out of any ruts they've fallen into. A Sagittarian enjoys talking to a brainy Virgo, but their expansive and spontaneous nature could eventually be restricted by the Virgo's need to think things through before taking action. When a Sagittarian gets together with a Capricorn, it's a case of optimism versus pessimism. While the Sagittarian's glass is half-full, the Capricorn's is always half-empty, and this causes many rows and possibly some ill feeling.

There could be lots of misunderstandings when a Sagittarian gets involved with one of the Water signs. A Sagittarian needs a bigger social circle than their family, whereas a Cancerian is quite happy surrounded by kith and kin. The Sagittarian need for independence won't go down well, either. It's like oil and water when a Sagittarian pairs up with a Scorpio. The Sagittarian is the roamer of the zodiac, whereas the Scorpio wants them where they can see them, in case they're up to no good. All will be well if the Sagittarian gets together with a strong-minded Piscean. In fact, they'll really enjoy one another's company. A Piscean who's lost in a world of their own, however, will soon leave them cold.

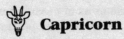

Capricorn

Despite their outward poise, a Capricorn is very easily hurt so they need to know their feelings won't be trampled on. There's least danger of that when they get together with a fellow Earth sign. A Capricorn adores a Taurean's deep sense of responsibility and they'll both work hard to create their ideal home. A Capricorn appreciates the methodical approach of a Virgo, but could feel deeply hurt by the Virgo's sharp tongue and caustic remarks. If two Capricorns team up, one of them must be demonstrative and openly affectionate, otherwise the relationship could be rather sterile and serious.

Capricorns also feel safe with members of the Water signs. When a Capricorn gets together with a Cancerian, they do their utmost to make their home a haven. They'll get great satisfaction from channelling their energies into bringing up a family. A Capricorn may be rather bemused by the depth and intensity of a Scorpio's emotions – Capricorns are too reserved to indulge in such drama themselves and it can make them feel uncomfortable. A no-nonsense Capricorn could be perplexed by an extremely vulnerable Piscean and won't know how to handle them. Should they give them a hanky or tell them to pull themselves together?

The Air signs can also make a Capricorn feel somewhat unsettled. They're fascinated by a Gemini's breadth of knowledge and endless chat, but they also find them superficial and rather flighty. In fact, the Capricorn probably doesn't trust the Gemini. A Capricorn feels far happier in the company of a Libran. Here's someone who seems much steadier emotionally and who can help the Capricorn to unwind after a hard day's work. It can be great or ghastly when a Capricorn sets their sights on an Aquarian. They understand each other provided the Aquarian isn't too unconventional, but the Capricorn feels uncomfortable and embarrassed by any displays of eccentricity, deliberate or not.

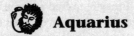

The Fire signs help to warm up the Capricorn, who can be rather remote and distant at times. A Capricorn admires the Arien's drive and initiative, but endlessly tells them to look before they leap and could become irritated when they don't take this sage advice. When a Capricorn gets together with a Leo, they won't need to worry about appearances – the Capricorn will feel justly proud of the smart Leo. However, they could wince when the bills come in and they discover how much those clothes cost. A Capricorn thinks a Sagittarian must have come from another planet – how can they be so relaxed and laid-back all the time? They have great respect for the Sagittarian's wisdom and philosophy, but they quickly become fed up with having to fit in around the Sagittarian's hectic social life.

Aquarius

Put an Aquarian with a fellow Air sign and they're happy. They thoroughly enjoy being with a lively Gemini and love discussing everything under the sun with them. They may not have a very exciting sex life, but their mental closeness will more than make up for it. The gentle charms of a Libran calms down an Aquarian when their nerves become frayed, although they disapprove of the Libran's innate tact and diplomacy – why can't they just say what they think, instead of sitting on the fence? With two Aquarians you never know what to expect, other than that they'll be great friends. They'll certainly do a lot of talking, but could spend more time debating esoteric ideas and abstract concepts.

An Aquarian likes all the Fire signs, although they find Ariens hard to fathom and can become exhausted by an Arien's endless supply of energy and enthusiasm. There are no such problems when an Aquarian pairs up with a Leo because they complement each other in many ways. The

Aquarian teaches objectivity to the Leo, who in return encourages the Aquarian to express their emotions more. An Aquarian thoroughly enjoys being with a Sagittarian because both of them hate being tied down. As a result, they respect one another's independence and will probably rarely see each other because of all their spare-time activities.

It's not quite so simple when an Aquarian joins forces with one of the Earth signs. An Aquarian will lock horns with a Taurean sooner or later, because neither of them is able to back down once a disagreement has started. The Aquarian will also feel very restricted by the Taurean's possessiveness. The Virgo's analytical approach to life intrigues the Aquarian but they'll sit up all night arguing the toss over everything, with each one convinced that they've got all the answers. When an Aquarian meets a Capricorn, they've got their work cut out for them if they're to find a happy medium between the erratic Aquarian and the conventional Capricorn.

An Aquarian feels out of their depth when they're with one of the Water signs. They simply don't understand what makes a Cancerian tick – why do they worry themselves sick over things that they can't change? The Aquarian finds it all most peculiar. They also find it difficult to understand a Scorpio who takes so many things so seriously. Although the Aquarian also has a list of topics that mean a lot to them, they're not the sort of things that hold the slightest interest for a Scorpio. It's more or less the same story with a Pisces, because their huge resources of emotion make the Aquarian feel uncomfortable and fill them with a strong desire to escape as fast as possible.

 **Pisces**

Relationships mean a lot to a sensitive Piscean, but they're easily misunderstood by many of the more robust signs. There are no such worries with the other Water signs, however. A Piscean loves being with a tender Cancerian who knows how to help them relax and feel safe. They really enjoy playing house together but the emotional scenes will blow the roof off. The relationship between a Piscean and a Scorpio can be quite spicy and sexy, but the Piscean is turned off if the Scorpio becomes too intense and dramatic. Two Pisceans feel safe with one another, but they'll push all their problems under the carpet unless one of them is more objective.

A Piscean also gets on well with the Earth signs, although with a few reservations. A Piscean takes comfort from being looked after by a protective Taurean, but after a while they could feel stifled by the Taurean's possessive and matter-of-fact attitude. The relationship between a Piscean and a Virgo starts off well but the Piscean could soon feel crushed by the Virgo's criticism and will need more emotional reassurance than the Virgo is able to give. A Piscean feels safe with a Capricorn because they're so dependable but in the end this may begin to bug them. It's not that they want the Capricorn to two-time them, more that they'd like a little unpredictability every now and then.

A Piscean is fascinated by the Air signs but their apparent lack of emotion could cause problems. A Piscean and a Gemini are terrific friends but could encounter difficulties as lovers. The Piscean's strong emotional needs are too much for the Gemini to handle – they'll feel as if they're drowning. The Piscean is on much firmer ground with a Libran, who'll go out of their way to keep the Piscean happy. Neither sign is good at facing up to any nasty truths, however. An Aquarian is too much for a sensitive Piscean, who views the world through rose-coloured specs. An Aquarian, on the other hand, has uncomfortably clear vision.

The Fire signs can cheer up a Piscean enormously, but any prolonged displays of emotion will make the Fire signs feel weighed down. The Piscean is fascinated by an Arien's exploits but could feel reluctant to join in. They'll also be easily hurt by some of the Arien's off-the-cuff remarks. When a Piscean pairs up with a Leo they appreciate the way the Leo wants to take charge and look after them. After a while, however, this could grate on them and they'll want to be more independent. A Piscean enjoys discussing philosophy and spiritual ideas with a Sagittarian – they can sit up half the night talking things through. The Sagittarian brand of honesty could hurt the Piscean at times, but they know this isn't malicious and will quickly forgive such outbursts.

 Aries

Because Ariens belong to the Fire element, they get on very well with their fellow Fire signs Leo and Sagittarius. All the same, an Arien getting together with a Leo will soon notice a distinct drop in their bank balance, because they'll enjoy going to all the swankiest restaurants and sitting in the best seats at the theatre. When an Arien pairs up with a Sagittarian, they'll compete over who drives the fastest car and has the most exciting holidays. When two Ariens get together the results can be combustible. Ideally, one Arien should be a lot quieter, otherwise they'll spend most of their time jostling for power. All these combinations are very sexy and physical.

Ariens also thrive in the company of the three Air signs – Gemini, Libra and Aquarius. Of the three, they get on best with Geminis, who share their rather childlike view of the world and also their sense of fun. An Arien and a Gemini enjoy hatching all sorts of ideas and schemes, even if they never get round to putting them into action. There's an exciting sense of friction between Aries and Libra, their opposite number in the zodiac. An Arien will be enchanted by the way their Libran caters to their every need, but may become impatient when the Libran

also wants to look after other people. An Arien will be capti-
vated by the originality of an Aquarian, although at times
they'll be driven mad by the Aquarian's eccentric approach
to life and the way they blow hot and cold in the bedroom.

Ariens don't do so well with the Earth signs – Taurus, Virgo
and Capricorn. The very careful, slightly plodding nature of a
typical Taurean can drive an Arien barmy at times, and
although they'll respect – and benefit from – the Taurean's
practical approach to life, it can still fill them with irritation.
An Arien finds it difficult to fathom a Virgo, because their
attitudes to life are diametrically opposed. An Arien likes to
jump in with both feet, while a Virgo prefers to take things
slowly and analyse every possibility before committing themselves. An Arien can get on quite well with a Capricorn,
because they're linked by their sense of ambition and their
earthy sexual needs.

An Arien is out of their depth with any of the Water signs –
Cancer, Scorpio and Pisces. They quickly become irritated by
the defensive Cancerian, although they'll love their cooking.
An Arien will enjoy a very passionate affair with a Scorpio, but
the Scorpio's need to know exactly what the Arien is up to
when their back is turned will soon cause problems and rifts.
Although an Arien may begin a relationship with a Pisces by
wanting to look after them and protect them from the harsh
realities of life, eventually the Piscean's extremely sensitive
nature may bring out the Arien's bullying streak.

Taurus

Taureans are literally in their element when they're with
Virgos or Capricorns who, like themselves, are Earth signs.
Two Taureans will get along very happily together, although
they could become so wedded to routine that they get stuck in

a rut. They may also encourage one another to eat too much. A Taurean will enjoy being with a Virgo, because they respect the Virgo's methodical nature. They'll also like encouraging their Virgo to relax and take life easy. Money will form a link between a Taurean and a Capricorn, with plenty of serious discussions on how to make it and what to do with it once they've got it. There will also be a strong sexual rapport, and the Taurean will encourage the more sensual side of the Capricorn.

The relationship between a Taurean and members of the Water element is also very good. A Taurean and a Cancerian will revel in one another's company and will probably be so happy at home that they'll rarely stir from their armchairs. They both have a strong need for emotional security and will stick together through thick and thin. There's plenty of passion when a Taurean pairs up with a Scorpio, although the faithful Taurean could become fed up with the Scorpio's jealous nature. They simply won't understand what they're being accused of, and their loyal nature will be offended by the very thought that they could be a two-timer. A Taurean will be delighted by a delicate Piscean, and will want to take care of such a vulnerable and sensitive creature.

Things become rather more complicated when a Taurean pairs up with an Arien, Leo or Sagittarian, all of whom are Fire signs. They have very little in common – Taureans like to take things slowly while Fire signs want to make things happen *now*. It's particularly difficult between a Taurean and an Arien – the careful Taurean will feel harried and rushed by the impetuous Arien. It's a little better when a Taurean gets together with a Leo, because they share a deep appreciation of the good things in life, although the Taurean will be horrified by the Leo's ability to spend money. Making joint decisions could be difficult, however, because they'll both stand their ground and refuse to budge. A Taurean and a Sagittarian simply don't understand each other – they're on such different wavelengths.

Any Taurean displays of possessiveness will make the independent Sagittarian want to run a mile.

Taureans are equally mystified by the Air signs – Gemini, Libra and Aquarius. What they see as the flightiness of Gemini drives them barmy – why can't the Gemini settle down and do one thing at a time? The Taurean will probably feel quite exhausted by the Gemini's many interests and bubbly character. Taurus and Libra are a surprisingly good pairing, because they share a need for beauty, luxury and love. This could end up costing the penny-wise Taurean quite a packet, but they'll have a deliciously romantic time along the way. Taurus and Aquarius are chalk and cheese, and neither one is prepared to meet the other one halfway. The Taurean need to keep tabs on their loved one's every movement will irritate the freedom-loving Aquarian, and there will be plenty of rows as a result.

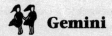 **Gemini**

One of the Air signs, Geminis get on very well with their fellow members of this element – Librans and Aquarians. Two Geminis are the astrological equivalent of double trouble – they chat nineteen to the dozen and revel in the company of someone who understands them so well. A Gemini delights in being with a Libran, because they enjoy the intellectual company and will benefit from the Libran's (usually) relaxed approach to life. They'll also learn to deal with their emotions more if a sympathetic Libran can guide them. Gemini and Aquarius is a very exciting pairing – the Gemini is encouraged to think deeply and knows that the Aquarian won't put up with any woolly ideas or fudged arguments.

Geminis also get on well with the three Fire signs – Aries, Leo and Sagittarius. A Gemini loves being with a racy, adventurous Arien, and together they enjoy keeping abreast of all the latest gossip and cultural developments. However, after the first flush of enthusiasm has worn off, the Gemini may find the Arien's strong need for sex rather hard to take. The Gemini gets on very well with a Leo. They delight in the Leo's affectionate nature and are amused by their need to have the best that money can buy – and they'll gladly share in the spoils. Gemini and Sagittarius are an excellent combination, because they sit opposite each other in the zodiac and so complement one another's character. The Gemini will be fascinated by the erudite and knowledgeable Sagittarian.

Gemini doesn't do so well with the Earth signs of Taurus and Capricorn, although they get on better with Virgo. The Gemini finds it difficult to understand a Taurean, because they see the world from such different viewpoints. The Gemini takes a more light-hearted approach and lives life at such a speed that they find it difficult to slow down to the more measured pace of a Taurean. The wonderfully dry Capricorn sense of humour is a source of constant delight to a Gemini. However, they're less taken with the Capricorn's streak of pessimism and their love of tradition. Of the three Earth signs, Gemini and Virgo are the most compatible. The Gemini shares the Virgo's brainpower and they have long, fascinating conversations.

When a Gemini gets together with the Water signs, the result can be enjoyable or puzzling. Gemini and Cancer have little in common, because the Gemini wants to spread their emotional and intellectual wings, whereas a Cancerian likes to stay close to home and has little interest in abstract ideas. Gemini finds Scorpio perplexing because they operate on such different levels. A Gemini tends to skim along the surface of things, so often deals with life on a superficial level, whereas a Scorpio likes to dig deep and has to have an emotional investment in everything they do. A Gemini appreciates the subtlety and sensitivity of a Piscean, but they're likely to make off-the-cuff comments that unwittingly hurt the Piscean.

🦀 Cancer

Cancerians revel in the company of their fellow Water signs of Scorpio and Pisces. When two Cancerians get together they could spend most of their time at home or eating – preferably both. They feel safe in the knowledge that they both have a strong need for love, but their innate Cancerian tenacity may mean they cling on to the relationship even if it's long past its best. A Cancerian is enchanted with a Scorpio, because at last they feel free to really let rip emotionally. However, the intuitive Cancerian should beware of soaking up the Scorpio's darker moods like a psychic sponge. A Cancerian will take one look at a delicate Piscean and want to invite them home for a good hot meal. All the Cancerian's protective instincts are aroused by a gentle Piscean, but their anger will also be aroused if it turns out the Piscean has been leading a double life behind their back.

Cancerians also find a great deal of comfort in the company of the Earth signs – Taurus, Virgo and Capricorn. Cancer and Taurus were made for each other – they both adore home comforts and they trust one another implicitly. The Cancerian loves making a cosy nest for their hard-working Taurean. A Cancerian finds a Virgo a more difficult proposition, especially emotionally. Whereas Cancer is all warm hugs and holding hands by the fire, Virgo prefers to read a book and reserve any displays of affection for the bedroom. Cancer and Capricorn are opposite numbers in the zodiac, so share a tremendous rapport. They also share the same values of home, tradition and family, and if anyone can help a Capricorn to relax and take life easy, it's a Cancerian.

Life becomes more difficult when it comes to a Cancerian's relationship with any of the Air signs. They simply don't understand one another. A Cancerian can't make a Gemini out. They feel confused by what they think of as the Gemini's flightiness and inability to stay in one place for long. They can also be easily hurt by the Gemini's difficulty in expressing their emotions. A Cancerian gets on much better with a Libran. They're both ambitious in their own ways and so have a great deal in common. The Cancerian enjoys the Libran's romantic nature, but the Cancerian tendency to cling doesn't go down well. A Cancerian regards a typical Aquarian as a being from another planet. They're hurt by the Aquarian's strong need for independence and dislike of having to account for their every action, and are dismayed and confused by the Aquarian's hot-and-cold attitude to sex.

The Fire signs of Aries, Leo and Sagittarius are also a potential source of bewilderment to the gentle Cancerian. They understand the drive and ambition of an Arien, but will be stung by their blunt speech and worried about their daredevil tendencies. What if they hurt themselves? A Cancerian gets on well with a Leo because they share a strong love of family and are both openly affectionate and loving. The Cancerian enjoys creating a home that the Leo can feel proud of. So far, so good, but the story isn't so simple when a Cancerian pairs up with a Sagittarian. They're too different to understand one another – the Cancerian wants to stay at home with the family while the Sagittarian has an instinctive need to roam the world. As a result, the Cancerian will be disappointed, and then hurt, when the Sagittarian's busy schedule takes them away from home too often.

 Leo

Leos adore the company of their fellow Fire signs, Ariens and Sagittarius. They understand one another and enjoy each other's spontaneous warmth and affection. A Leo is amused by the exuberance and impulsiveness of an Arien, and they enjoy being persuaded to let their hair down a bit and not worry too much about appearances. A Leo enjoys the dash and vitality of a Sagittarian, although they may feel irritated if they can never get hold of them on the phone or the Sagittarian is always off doing other things. Two Leos together either love or loathe one another. One of them should be prepared to take a back seat otherwise they'll both be vying for the limelight all the time.

The three Air signs of Gemini, Libra and Aquarius all get on well with Leos. When a Leo pairs up with a Gemini, you can expect lots of laughter and plenty of fascinating conversations. The demonstrative Leo is able to help the Gemini be more openly affectionate and loving. Leo and Libra is a great combination, and the Leo is enchanted by the Libran's fair-minded attitude. Both signs love luxury and all the good things in life but their bank managers may not be so pleased by the amount of the money they manage to spend. Leo and Aquarius sit opposite one another across the horoscope, so they already have a great deal in common. They're fascinated by one another but they're both very stubborn, so any disputes between them usually end in stalemate because neither is prepared to concede any ground.

Leos don't really understand the Earth signs. Although Leos admire their practical approach to life, they find it rather restricting. A Leo enjoys the sensuous and hedonistic side of a Taurean's character but may become frustrated by their fear of change. Leo and Virgo have very little in common, especially when it comes to food – the Leo wants to tuck in at all the best restaurants while the Virgo is worried about the state of the kitchens, the number of calories and the size of the bill. A Leo respects the Capricorn's desire to support their family and approves of their need to be seen in the best possible light, but they feel hurt by the Capricorn's difficulty in showing their feelings.

When a Leo gets together with one of the Water signs –

Cancer, Scorpio or Pisces – they'll enjoy the sexual side of the relationship but could eventually feel stifled by all that Watery emotion. A Leo and a Cancerian adore making a home together and both dote on their children. The Leo also likes comforting their vulnerable Cancerian – provided this doesn't happen too often. A Leo and a Scorpio will be powerfully attracted to one another, but power could also pull them apart – who's going to wear the trousers? They'll also lock horns during rows and both of them will refuse to back down. A Leo delights in a sophisticated Piscean, but may become irritated by their indecision and jangly nerves.

Compatibility in Love and Sex at a glance

F M	♈	♉	♊	♋	♌	♍	♎	♏	♐	♑	♒	♓
♈	8	5	9	7	9	4	7	8	9	7	7	3
♉	6	8	4	10	7	8	8	7	3	8	2	8
♊	8	2	7	3	8	7	9	4	9	4	9	4
♋	5	10	4	8	6	5	6	8	2	9	2	8
♌	9	8	9	7	7	4	9	6	8	7	9	6
♍	4	8	6	4	4	7	6	7	7	9	4	4
♎	7	8	10	7	8	5	9	6	9	6	10	6
♏	7	9	4	7	6	6	7	10	5	6	5	7
♐	9	4	10	4	9	7	8	4	9	6	9	5
♑	7	8	4	9	6	8	6	4	4	8	4	5
♒	8	6	9	4	9	4	9	6	8	7	8	2
♓	7	6	7	9	6	7	6	9	7	5	4	9

1 = the pits
10 = the peaks

Key

♈ – Aries
♉ – Taurus
♊ – Gemini
♋ – Cancer
♌ – Leo
♍ – Virgo

♎ – Libra
♏ – Scorpio
♐ – Sagittarius
♑ – Capricorn
♒ – Aquarius
♓ – Pisces

Compatibility in Friendship at a glance

F⟋M	♈	♉	♊	♋	♌	♍	♎	♏	♐	♑	♒	♓
♈	8	5	10	5	9	3	7	8	9	6	8	5
♉	6	9	6	10	7	8	7	6	4	9	3	9
♊	9	3	9	4	9	8	10	5	10	5	10	6
♋	6	9	4	9	5	4	6	9	4	10	3	9
♌	10	7	9	6	9	4	8	6	9	6	9	7
♍	5	9	8	4	4	8	5	8	8	10	5	6
♎	8	9	10	8	8	6	9	5	9	6	10	7
♏	7	8	5	8	7	7	6	9	4	5	6	8
♐	9	5	10	4	10	8	8	4	10	7	9	6
♑	6	9	5	10	6	6	5	5	4	9	5	6
♒	9	6	10	5	9	5	9	7	9	5	9	3
♓	6	7	6	10	6	8	7	9	8	6	4	10

1 = the pits
10 = the peaks

Key

♈ – Aries		♎ – Libra	
♉ – Taurus		♏ – Scorpio	
♊ – Gemini		♐ – Sagittarius	
♋ – Cancer		♑ – Capricorn	
♌ – Leo		♒ – Aquarius	
♍ – Virgo		♓ – Pisces	

HOBBIES AND THE STARS

What do you do in your spare time? If you're looking for some new interests to keep you occupied in 2000, read on to discover which hobbies are ideal for your Sun sign.

 Virgo

One of your favourite pastimes is to keep up to date with your health. You're fascinated by medical matters and you enjoy reading books telling you how to keep fit. You may even try out all the latest eating regimes, hoping that you'll find one that suits you perfectly. This interest in health means you're keen to eat well, and you could enjoy growing your own vegetables. Even cultivating a few herbs in a windowbox will give you a sense of achievement and you'll be pleased to think they are doing you good. You have tremendous patience so you might enjoy fiddly hobbies that require great dexterity, such as knitting, needlepoint and sewing. You might also enjoy painting designs on china and glass.

♎ Libra

Libra is a very sensual sign, so any hobbies that appeal to your senses are bound to go down well. You love delicious smells so you might enjoy learning about aromatherapy, so you can cure yourself of minor ailments and also create your own bath oils. You could also get a big thrill out of making your own cosmetics or soaps, and you might become so good at them that you give them away as gifts. You take great pride in looking good, so you enjoy visiting your favourite shops and keeping up with the latest fashions. Music is one of your great loves and you might play an instrument or sing. If not, you certainly appreciate other people's musical talents and you enjoy going to concerts and recitals.

 **Scorpio**

Whatever hobbies you choose, they have to mean a lot to you. You simply aren't interested in activities that don't carry an emotional meaning for you and you'd rather not bother with them at all. One pastime that's dear to the hearts of most Scorpios is wine-tasting. You might enjoy teaching yourself all about wine, either with the help of some good books or simply by drinking whatever appeals to you. You're fascinated by mysteries, and you could enjoy reading lots of whodunits or books on true crimes. You are also intrigued by things that go bump in the night, and you can't resist going on ghost hunts or visiting famous places that are known to be haunted.

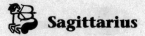 **Sagittarius**

You're one of the great collectors of the zodiac, whether you know it or not. You may not think that you collect anything at all, but other people will take one look at all your books and beg to disagree with you. Reading is one of your great pleasures in life and you're always buying books on your latest enthusiasms. Travel is something else that appeals to you, and you love planning where you're going to go next on holiday. You like to keep active and you enjoy outdoor sports in particular. Horse-riding is a classic Sagittarian activity, and you enjoy going to the races and having a little flutter. You also like activities that present you with a challenge – you're always determined to beat it!

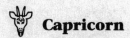 **Capricorn**

If you're a typical Capricorn you often take life rather seriously, so it's important for you to have lots of spare-time activities that allow you to relax. However, you've got to find the time first, and that means stopping work rather than burning the candle at both ends. Something that might appeal to you is rock-climbing, and you'll enjoy planning the strategy of how you're going to get to the top. Even a gentle walk amid mountain scenery does you a lot of good and helps you to relax. You're a very practical sign and you enjoy gardening. Not only does it help to ground you, you also like growing your own fruit and vegetables and then comparing the prices with those in the shops. Music helps you to unwind, and you'll love going to the opera or a glittering concert.

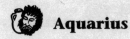 **Aquarius**

Most Aquarians have such a wide range of interests that almost anything is bound to appeal to you. You may go through phases, immersing yourself in one hobby for years until another one takes your fancy. However, you are only interested in activities that keep you intellectually stimulated and that teach you more about the world. You may go to lots of different evening classes, and you might even study for a degree in your spare time. Eastern philosophy could appeal, and you might also be an active campaigner for human rights. Astrology is a big hit with many Aquarians, and you'll enjoy teaching yourself all about it. Group activities are another interest, and you're an avid member of all sorts of organizations and societies.

 **Pisces**

Anything artistic or creative is perfect for you, because you have abundant gifts at your disposal. Painting, drawing, writing poetry and dancing are all classic Piscean pastimes. In fact, you may feel rather fed up or stifled when you can't express yourself creatively. When you want to escape from the world, you love going to the cinema or the theatre. You're a Water sign so you enjoy any activities connected with water, such as swimming or other forms of water sports. Many Pisceans enjoy gardening, and you'll especially like having some form of water feature in your garden even if it's very modest. You're very musical, and would enjoy learning to play an instrument if you can't already do so. You might also like using your psychic talents, perhaps by learning to read the tarot or runes.

Aries

Ariens love to keep active, so you aren't interested in any sort of hobby that's very sedentary or that keeps you glued to the sofa. You much prefer being kept busy, especially if it's out of doors. You also have a strong sense of adventure and a great love of speed, so one hobby that's right up your street is motor-racing. You might be lucky enough to be the driver, or you could be a spectator shouting yourself hoarse from the stands, but this is a sport you love. Speaking of sports, anything that's competitive and which threatens to knock the stuffing out of you will also suit you down to the ground. Rugby, football and baseball all fit the bill, and you might also enjoy martial arts and Eastern forms of exercise such as T'ai Chi.

 **Taurus**

You belong to one of the Earth signs, so it's no surprise that many Taureans were born with green fingers. You always feel better when you can be out in the fresh air, especially if you're in beautiful surroundings, so you adore gardening. Even if you're not keen on wielding a spade yourself you'll enjoy appreciating other people's efforts. Cooking is something that has enormous appeal for you and you enjoy creating gourmet meals, especially if the ingredients include your favourite foods. You also enjoy visiting swanky restaurants, although some of the gilt will be wiped off the gingerbread if you don't think you're getting value for money. Members of your sign are renowned for having beautiful voices so you might enjoy singing in a choir or on your own.

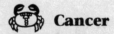 Gemini

One of your favourite ways of passing the time is to curl up with a good book. You'll eagerly read newspapers and magazines as well, and you always attempt crosswords and other sorts of puzzle even if you don't always finish them. Jigsaws intrigue you, especially if you can do something else at the same time, such as listening to music or watching the TV. You belong to a sign that doesn't like sitting still for long and you absolutely thrive on keeping active, so it's important for you to enjoy hobbies that make sure you get plenty of exercise. Tennis is a classic Gemini sport because it involves a lot of skill but it also boosts your social life. Dancing is another activity that helps you to keep fit while having a really good time.

Cancer

Home comforts are very important to you, so you spend a lot of time and money on making sure your home is the way you want it. You may enjoy reading magazines on interior design or you could be glued to all the DIY programmes on TV, adapting the best ideas for your own home. One of your greatest skills is cooking, because you belong to a sign that derives enormous emotional comfort from food. You take pleasure in cooking for your loved ones and you probably have a big collection of cookery books to provide you with endless inspiration. Water sports could appeal to you, especially if they involve visiting your favourite beach. You might also enjoy fishing, particularly if you can do it by moonlight.

Leo

You have a host of artistic skills and talents at your fingertips because you belong to the one of the most creative signs in the zodiac. One of your favourite hobbies is amateur dramatics, because most Leos adore being in the limelight. You may even have thought about becoming a professional actor because you enjoy treading the boards so much. You might also enjoy dancing, whether you go to regular classes or you simply love tripping the light fantastic with your partner. Travel appeals to you, especially if you can visit luxurious hotels in hot parts of the world. However, you're not very keen on roughing it! Clothes are very important to you, so you enjoy shopping for the latest fashions and you may also be an accomplished dressmaker.

THE YEAR 2000

 Friends and Lovers

It's quite a mixed bag for your relationships in 2000. Major changes are starting to affect your family life, and these could take some getting used to. They are especially likely if you were born between 2 and 8 September. You might have to sort out some difficulties with someone or you could have to cope with an enforced separation. Although it will be difficult to deal with disruptions in your domestic and family life, once the dust has settled you'll realize that they were a blessing in disguise. You might learn some very important lessons about the way certain people behave in a crisis, or you could discover that you have considerable inner strength.

As the year begins, you're enjoying a wonderful time with close partners. Your sex life may be flourishing as never before, and you'll enjoy this period of emotional intimacy. You may also realize that a certain someone means a lot more to you than you'd ever imagined, and that perhaps it's time you did something about it.

You'll be fascinated by people who come from a different walk of life this year, especially between February and late

June. In fact, the more differences there are between you, the more intrigued you'll be. If you're taking off on holiday you could have a romance that adds to your store of happy memories.

Older friends and relatives could be rather hard-going between August and September, and you may find it a struggle if you have to spend a lot of time with them. You might feel that they're being rather critical of you, or that your relationship is going through a sticky patch. Luckily, this tricky period won't last long.

Health

Variety is the spice of life this year, and the more adventures you can enjoy the better you'll feel. It will do you the world of good to have lots of short breaks and changes of scene throughout the year. Although several holidays in 2000 are exactly what the doctor ordered, your bank manager may take a different view! So at least try to arrange weekends away in which you can visit friends and family, even if you can't afford to take off into the wide blue yonder whenever the urge comes upon you.

As a Virgo you belong to the most health-conscious sign of all and you should certainly take good care of yourself this year. There will be times when you don't have as much energy as you'd like, and this will be when you're especially susceptible to germs and infections. So try to keep well away from people who are coughing and sneezing. You could also be prey to mysterious symptoms that are difficult for your doctor to diagnose or which come and go with monotonous regularity.

Although these will probably turn out to be nothing at all, you should still follow up any symptoms that you're worried about.

If you want to take more exercise this year, bear in mind that you'll be easily bored. So try to do things that keep you fully occupied or which have a social element, so you can chat to friends while you keep fit. Otherwise, you'll find it hard to keep up the good work. Swimming and other water-based forms of exercise will be especially good for you.

You could also become interested in changing your diet. You might be attracted to vegetarianism if you're currently a committed carnivore, or you could experiment with other healthy ways of eating.

 **Money**

If you want to make the most of your money in 2000, the secret is to invest as much as possible at the start of the year. If you were wise you began salting away your spare cash in 1999, and by now you should be seeing some rewards for all your efforts. Don't worry if you didn't start a savings scheme last year because it's never too late to begin!

It's a great year for seeking financial advice, especially if you aren't absolutely sure what to do for the best. Talk to a financial adviser or your bank manager about pensions, insurance schemes, tax planning or anything else that is appropriate. A little foresight could bring you big dividends later on. The best times to seek financial advice are the first six weeks of the year, and then between late June and late September. From October onwards you may find it slightly difficult to set the ball rolling or to make things happen. There could be delays or you may wonder whether you're being given the best advice.

You're feeling flush in March and April, and again in September and October. These are all good times to spend money, especially if you're buying something that will bring you pleasure. Keep a close eye on joint accounts between March and April, and make sure that they're working as you'd like. This is also a good opportunity to discuss financial matters with your partner and sort out any potential hiccups before they turn into problems.

Career

Get set for a really busy year! It also promises to be a very successful one where your career is concerned, and you could find yourself basking in the limelight in 2000 when your talents are finally recognized and celebrated. You might also discover that you've got friends in high places this year, perhaps when someone in authority pulls a few strings on your behalf or you manage to get on the right side of a boss or superior.

Even so, you must be prepared to put in some hard work because unfortunately these rewards won't simply land in your lap. You might have to take on extra responsibilities or duties, or you may have to hold the fort when other people aren't available. Your personal life could have to take a back seat while all this is going on, but such sacrifices will be worth it in the long run.

Your working surroundings could be rather unpredictable this year. There might be changes to where you work, perhaps when you move offices. You may also have to deal with colleagues and customers who are erratic, eccentric or difficult to cope with. Someone could be very elusive or they might behave in ways that you don't expect. You'll have to be flexible if you want to stay on top of the situation. Try to vary your daily routine as much as possible, otherwise you could quickly become bored or fed up.

If you decide to change jobs, try to make sure you're being realistic about your prospects. Otherwise, you could find that you're looking for the dream job that doesn't exist, or you might take on a job that isn't all it's cracked up to be. Jobs connected with technology, New Age interests and the fashion and cosmetics industries will go very well this year.

Your Day by Day Guide

JANUARY AT A GLANCE

Love	♥ ♥ ♥ ♥ ♥
Money	£
Career	💻 💻 💻 💻 💻
Health	☼ ☼ ☼ ☼ ☼

• Saturday 1 January •

Happy New Year! You're starting 2000 in a strong position because you feel fit, full of energy and you're raring to go. You feel quietly confident about the year ahead and, not one to leave much to chance, you've probably already mapped out the direction in which you're heading. Physically, mentally and emotionally, you're equipped to reach your desired destination this year.

• Sunday 2 January •

What a productive day! You can get a lot of jobs done around the house that you didn't have time to get round to before. You want to simplify your life and get rid of all the old clutter to create a more ordered and calm environment. It's time to get rid of anything that's past its sell-by date and which you no longer have any use for if you're serious about streamlining your life.

• Monday 3 January •

You're feeling much more positive about your domestic life and seeing your home in a completely new light today. Beautifying your surroundings has a wonderfully uplifting effect and could inspire you to do some entertaining or invite some good friends over to your place. Why not treat yourself to some new things for your home to add the last finishing touches?

• Tuesday 4 January •

It seems that it's not only on the home front that you're making changes, and your family in particular may wonder what's got into you. It could be time to tell a close relative a few home truths if you want to resolve the difficulties between you and clear the air. They may not like what you have to say but at least the tensions of the past can finally be resolved.

• Wednesday 5 January •

You may have been in two minds about a close partnership recently, but you can put any doubts you had behind you. What you now realize is how committed you are to this relationship, but you'll need to have a heart-to-heart to establish how you both really feel. At least for your part, you've come to the point where you're willing to give it your best shot.

• Thursday 6 January •

Ready for an exciting new development? You take on a more prominent role today and your increased visibility gives you the chance to show off your skills and abilities. This is particularly good news if you've been hiding your light under a bushel and not allowing yourself to shine. Gaining the recognition you deserve will do wonders for your confidence and self-esteem.

• Friday 7 January •

You've got the Midas touch today, and things that you've been working hard to achieve will suddenly fall into place. Everything you do goes well and you'll automatically attract the support you need. You might think there's a catch to all this and that it sounds too good to be true, but don't forget that it's because you laid the groundwork that all of this is now possible. Congratulations!

• *Saturday 8 January* •

You'll be giving some thought to your everyday life today and thinking about how to create more free time. If you're a typical Virgo, you like a certain amount of order, but if things become too regimented you can box yourself in and find yourself trapped in too tight a schedule. Once you allow the other sides of yourself to be expressed, you'll feel more in balance.

• *Sunday 9 January* •

Anyone visiting you today is likely to find a Do Not Disturb sign on your front door! Curling up with a loved one at home is your idea of heaven. You're feeling at your most romantic and amorous, and all you want to do is shut yourselves away from the world and enjoy some time together. Looks like you're all set for a memorable day.

• *Monday 10 January* •

Floating on Cloud Nine? Your feet probably won't touch the ground today and your normal capacity to concentrate will seem to have deserted you. Your mind is all over the place at the moment so you might as well give up trying to keep everything under control. Your feelings are definitely in charge and, at least for today, you're better off giving them a free rein.

• *Tuesday 11 January* •

You're totally baffled by the way you're feeling today and you may even come to the conclusion that there are some things that even a Virgo can't analyse! The heart has emotions and compulsions that our rational side finds impossible to fathom, so you might as well give up trying to understand the depth of your emotions. Talking about how you feel might help.

• *Wednesday 12 January* •

Although you don't exactly feel cool, calm and collected, you are feeling more self-possessed and you are feeling more in touch with the state of your emotions. Taking a step back from everything will give you the breathing space you need to take stock of the current emotional climate. Once you've put your feelings into perspective, you'll feel a lot more able to cope.

• *Thursday 13 January* •

You've got bags of energy today and you feel inspired to do something out of the ordinary. If there's a part of your life which feels dreary or as if you are on a treadmill, now is the time to see how you can make some changes in that area. Perhaps something has outlived its purpose and no longer serves you. If so, you may now be ready to pluck up the courage to let it go.

• *Friday 14 January* •

You'll have to be very careful to say what you mean today because otherwise you could end up at cross-purposes with a loved one or partner. The problem is that one of you is operating on a short fuse and likely to explode at the slightest provocation. Take a deep breath and keep your cool if you want to avoid a scene. Hopefully, this person takes their cue from you, and you can then sort out your differences.

• Saturday 15 January •

Duty comes before pleasure today because there are certain commitments that you have to honour. You may have to spend a few hours working on something that you didn't have time to finish during the week, and you can't really relax until you've got it out of the way. Having to buckle down to work isn't so much of a chore as it sounds – you might even find it therapeutic!

• Sunday 16 January •

You're able to see any recent hiccups as a useful learning curve and chalk the whole episode down to experience today. With hindsight, you can now make sense of the past and recognize that sooner or later the things that once seemed confused become clearer. Feeling on more solid ground gives you the confidence to be more assertive where a certain person is concerned.

• Monday 17 January •

You're torn between erring on the side of caution and taking a risk today. Although your Virgoan nature may favour being more circumspect, something tells you you may be short-changing yourself by playing it safe. You'll have to use your powers of reasoning to weigh up the pros and cons but, in the end, you may simply have to take a leap of faith.

• Tuesday 18 January •

Much as you'd love to enjoy a self-indulgent day at home today and not have to deal with the outside world, it looks as though there are other plans in store for you. A situation at work means that you have to think on your feet and come up with a solution fast. As stressful as this sounds, if you can keep your nerve you'll do a first-class job and get the praise you deserve.

• Wednesday 19 January •

A chance remark gives you a whole new perspective on the way you've been behaving with a colleague or business associate. What you realize is that you may need to be more forward thinking in your approach if you're to get the best out of your working relationship. Some of the methods you've been using may now be more of a hindrance than a help.

• Thursday 20 January •

Your practical and realistic side may give way today to a more intuitive and idealistic part of your nature. Give yourself plenty of scope to explore what you'd really love to do and what you instinctively know is possible. You may realize that your way of thinking has limited you, and that you actually have a lot more room to manoeuvre than you imagined.

• Friday 21 January •

You may have to bow to the wishes of others today and bide your time until you can get your opinions across. There's no point in forcing the issue because things will go much more smoothly if you choose your moment carefully. Your ideas are gathering momentum, and it's only a matter of time before you'll have the chance to do your own thing.

• Saturday 22 January •

Sparks are flying all around you today but somehow you manage to keep out of the rumpus. You'd much rather mind your own business than become embroiled in a heated debate that really has nothing to do with you. Others may provoke you in an attempt to draw you in, and although it will upset you to witness such a commotion, you owe it to yourself to stand your ground.

• *Sunday 23 January* •

You may find yourself picking up the pieces today and being the shoulder that someone wants to cry on. If you're true to your sign, you can maintain your composure when everyone else is falling apart – and that's just what you may be called to do. Although you're willing to offer any support or advice that's necessary, try to maintain a healthy distance.

• *Monday 24 January* •

You can kiss goodbye to any routine today when unforeseen circumstances throw you off course. Try to go with the flow as much as possible if you want to stay on top of things and don't allow the uncertainty to worry you. There's a rhyme and reason to the change of plan and although it may not make sense now, everything will soon fall into place.

• *Tuesday 25 January* •

Someone you're devoted to is particularly demanding today and you may need to think twice before giving them all your time and energy. It's important that you keep something in reserve, otherwise you'll soon be running on empty and no good to anyone. You may be able to work out a compromise which gives you the chance to look after both of you.

• *Wednesday 26 January* •

There's a strong likelihood of a reshuffle on the work front and this may necessitate a change in the day-to-day running of your professional life. Your challenge is to see how much of the status quo you can keep without throwing the baby out with the bathwater. Fortunately, everything is fairly clear cut and you won't need to deliberate for long on how to restructure things.

• *Thursday 27 January* •

You could have a pleasant surprise today and discover that your bank balance is in a healthier state than you realized. You might even receive a windfall from an unexpected source, which will come in more than handy. Whatever the reason, you are definitely feeling more flush and, given the recent financial fluctuations, this couldn't have come at a better time.

• *Friday 28 January* •

You're in danger of going into mental overload today because there are so many issues you have to deal with. The fact that they're all equally important makes it almost impossible to put them in order of priority, which means you're having to juggle an unmanageable amount of balls in the air. You really don't need to cope all alone, so get some help – fast!

• *Saturday 29 January* •

At last you can make up for lost time and put pleasure before business. This is a wonderful day to have a get-together with people you wish you could see more often. Even if you don't do anything special, simply being together in a carefree and joyous atmosphere will be just the tonic you need to revitalize yourself.

• *Sunday 30 January* •

If you're a typical Virgo you're probably quite good at following a keep fit regime, and you probably have all the books to prove it. You may need to take stock of how well you look after yourself today and decide if there are any areas you could improve on. If diet and exercise aren't high on your agenda, this would be a good time to start a healthier lifestyle.

• *Monday 31 January* •

You're in such an upbeat mood today that the air around you is positively crackling! You're able to channel all that mental energy into some very productive areas and get more done than you have in a long time. You have a very optimistic feeling about the outcome of one particular project and, if you're right, the success will be all yours as it has your name written all over it.

FEBRUARY AT A GLANCE

Love	♥ ♥ ♥ ♥
Money	£ $ £
Career	💻 💻 💻 💻 💻
Health	☼ ☼ ☼ ☼ ☼

• *Tuesday 1 February* •

Ready to be paid a compliment? You'll impress others today with your resourcefulness and self-motivation, so allow yourself a pat on the back and recognize how much people believe in you. You may not like to blow your own trumpet, but you'd be doing yourself a disservice if you failed to acknowledge your skills and strengths.

• *Wednesday 2 February* •

If you're planning a holiday today you've got no shortage of ideas as to where you want to go. In your current mood, you'd much rather choose somewhere expensive and exotic – cheap and cheerful may have its compensations, but right now you're tempted to splash out. Unless you really do have to watch the purse strings, why not treat yourself to the best?

• *Thursday 3 February* •

You can count your blessings today because things simply fall into your lap without you having to lift a finger. Mind you, it's not as if you haven't prepared the ground for good fortune to come your way. The harvest you're currently reaping is a product of hard work plus a dash of serendipity thrown in for good measure. All you have to do now is sit back and enjoy the fruits of your labour.

• *Friday 4 February* •

This is a good day to sign any agreements or enter into negotiations of any kind. You're able to make sure that everything is straightforward and clear-cut, and that nothing is left to chance. You can work well with others to achieve a mutually beneficial arrangement and you can trust the people you're dealing with, so the outcome is bound to be favourable.

• *Saturday 5 February* •

Today feels like a breath of fresh air and it seems as if you're seeing everything with new eyes. You're aware that something in you is changing for the better and it's altering your whole perspective. This would be the perfect day to forget your normal routine and do something completely different. Why not discover a place you've never been to before?

• *Sunday 6 February* •

Breaking out of your routine has given you a new lease of life and you're feeling on top of the world. You're thinking ahead and making plans for the future that will give you more freedom and independence. Having greater autonomy will not only allow you to be more your own person, it'll also give you the opportunity to feel more in charge of your life.

• *Monday 7 February* •

Talk about leaving no stone unturned! A loved one or partner may need some reassurance from you today. With all the changes currently taking place they may wonder where they fit into the scheme of things, and they may even wonder if there's a place for them at all. This gives you the chance to re-evaluate where you stand emotionally, and how you can take your relationship forward.

• *Tuesday 8 February* •

What you would ideally like to get done today and what you achieve in reality are two separate issues. Unfortunately, events conspire to frustrate you in your attempts to get ahead, and there's very little you can do about it. Try to divert your attention to something that you can at least make some headway with, and do your best to contain your frustration.

• *Wednesday 9 February* •

Thank goodness you're now able to channel all your energies into whatever you really want to do. Yesterday's hold-up tested your patience, but order has been restored and you can now get on with the agenda you've set yourself. You can be a hard taskmaster – especially to yourself – and yet you know you can't afford to slouch if you're to achieve your goals.

• *Thursday 10 February* •

Trust your intuition today where a business partner or associate is concerned. They may be saying one thing and thinking something else, and you might suspect they're not being honest with you. It's better to confront the issue rather than give them the benefit of the doubt, and if you put two and two together it won't take you long to work out what they're playing at.

• *Friday 11 February* •

If a loved one or partner has been evasive of late, you can pin them down today and find out why they've been avoiding certain issues. Although they might be reticent at first, your patience and non-threatening manner will soon put them at ease and help them to open up. They'll probably be relieved and grateful that you gave them the chance to get things off their chest.

• *Saturday 12 February* •

You're brimming over with new ideas today but if you want to keep up with yourself, you're going to need to write them down before they disappear into the ether. Take time out today to slow down and put your thoughts into some kind of order, otherwise you'll end up with so much mental clutter that you won't be able to think straight. Relax!

• *Sunday 13 February* •

You can't help keeping busy today – even though nothing is really that important. It's simply that you feel you should be doing something productive and not sitting around taking life easy. Your mind is probably working overtime, and trying to still it and focus your attention on more leisurely pursuits is an uphill battle. Even so, try to find a balance or you will soon feel exhausted.

• *Monday 14 February* •

Happy Valentine's Day! You might surprise yourself by the depth of your emotions today and wonder what prompted such strong feelings. You're setting the stage for a romantic evening and whether you've just met, or you've been together for a while, you're determined to make this a very special occasion for you and your partner.

• *Tuesday 15 February* •

You have a wonderful, warm feeling today and people can't help but notice your inner glow. You're happy and content with yourself and, if you spend the day with friends, you'll feel especially open towards them and will enjoy every minute of their company. You're at your most sociable and you may even meet someone new that you form an instant rapport with.

• *Wednesday 16 February* •

If you're involved in any kind of group activity today, you will feel extremely comfortable and at ease with everyone. You will be able to express your emotions in a fluent and accessible way, and others will be very receptive to what you have to say. By the same token, you are equally open and sympathetic to other points of view, and feel delighted that you can all work so well together.

• *Thursday 17 February* •

Even though as a Virgo you can probably work quite happily on your own, you feel more at home working as part of a team at the moment. You will all get on like a house on fire because you're all on the same wavelength. Even when you don't see eye to eye, you're easily able to resolve your difficulties. It's not every day that you find a winning formula like this one, so enjoy it!

• *Friday 18 February* •

Hold tight, because you're about to go into romantic orbit. You could be all lined up for a hot date if you manage to keep your nerve and everything goes according to plan. Someone who's been sending you covert signals has finally plucked up the courage to ask you out. Or maybe it's you that's doing the pursuing, after doing your best to pretend you weren't interested. Have fun!

• *Saturday 19 February* •

'Over the moon' is probably the best way of describing your state of mind today. You're feeling so excited about a recent development that your normal composure has flown straight out of the window. You feel as if you'll burst if you don't share your good news, so spend some time with a dear friend and spread a little happiness!

• *Sunday 20 February* •

Yesterday's exuberance has probably worn you out and you might actually feel like a day to yourself today just to recharge your batteries. Think of something nice to do that you particularly enjoy, such as soaking in a warm bath or cooking a delicious meal. Allow your thoughts to wander where they will and take time catch up with yourself. You deserve a little breather!

• *Monday 21 February* •

If you managed to give yourself a few treats yesterday, you're bound to be feeling very calm and relaxed today. You're probably wondering why you don't spoil yourself more often, and this could be a good time to resolve to do just that in the future. If you do decide to pamper yourself more regularly, you'll be amazed at the difference in the way you feel.

• *Tuesday 22 February* •

You may be involved in a tug of war over a financial matter today, and although you want to play it fair, somebody is definitely not so honourably intentioned. It could be that there's more at stake than money, and if there's an emotional connection between you, it is bound to muddy the water. Try to keep your head and not be provoked.

• *Wednesday 23 February* •

If you were able to keep your cool yesterday, you should be feeling relieved now that you managed to avert a major drama. Relationships run more smoothly today and you feel especially in harmony with one particular person. Being on the same wavelength makes for such an effortless communication that you could almost dispense with words!

• *Thursday 24 February* •

You're in a bit of a dream today, which makes it hard for you to concentrate or get anything done. Even so, it's a fantastic day for doing something creative or imaginative. It's almost as if you've absented yourself for the day so that you can float a few things in your mind and see where they lead. Anyone trying to get through to you will probably give up, as they'll soon realize that your mind is somewhere else.

• *Friday 25 February* •

You come up with a brilliant solution today to a problem that's been bothering you. It literally pops into your head when you least expect it, and now that you've found it, the rest seems like a piece of cake. Once you've discussed your proposal with the relevant parties, you will then be able to put it to the test and see if it's as good as you think it is.

• *Saturday 26 February* •

Home improvements are top of the agenda today and you probably already have a list of jobs to be done that you can't wait to get your teeth into. Although you can't make sweeping changes overnight, you're slowly getting your home the way you want it. If you're a typical Virgo and a bit of a perfectionist, you will want to take your time but the effort will be worth it in the end.

• *Sunday 27 February* •

Talk about all systems go! If you've devoted the whole weekend to the house, far from wearing you out, it's positively energizing you. Seeing something change for the better has a very uplifting effect on you and makes you feel that you're doing something both creative and useful. It's almost as if you're getting an overhaul at the same time as your home!

• *Monday 28 February* •

Someone who depends on you to be straight needs your advice today. The problem is that although they want the truth, they may not like it when they hear it. There's no point in sugaring the pill and making the facts more palatable, because they'll see straight through it. There's nothing for it but to tell it like it is. However, that doesn't mean a little tact won't come in useful.

• *Tuesday 29 February* •

You can move mountains today and that's exactly what you intend to do. You're fuelled with ambition and determined to make your mark. You've been waiting for this moment, and now is the time to show how resolute you can be when something matters enough. Others may have to lift their jaws off the ground when they see how assertive you can be when you want something.

MARCH AT A GLANCE

Love	♥ ♥ ♥ ♥ ♥
Money	£ $ £ $
Career	💻 💻 💻
Health	☼ ☼ ☼

• *Wednesday 1 March* •

You feel very attuned to a partner or loved one today and you're able to discuss some sensitive issues without either of you hitting the roof. Neither of you has an axe to grind, but you do want to resolve any differences that may exist between you. As long as you're prepared to hear each other out, you will reach an understanding.

• *Thursday 2 March* •

You could hear from someone today whom you haven't seen for ages. You may even have thought you'd lost touch with them. You'll be delighted at how quickly you're able to re-kindle your friendship and how happy you are to speak to each other again. The timing of their re-entry into your life is perfect, because you're in need of what they have to offer.

• *Friday 3 March* •

A break in your routine comes as a welcome relief today because you're beginning to flag and your boredom threshold is at an all-time low. Certain aspects of your everyday life have become repetitive, and you need to tackle something new that occupies your attention and which you can get your teeth into. If you make a concerted effort to explore new possibilities, it won't take long before you hit on something.

• *Saturday 4 March* •

You're in the mood for fun and laughter today, and the more friends you can get together with, the more scope you'll have to enjoy yourself. Being with people that bring out the best in you is uplifting and will do wonders for your self-esteem. Although Virgos aren't necessarily extrovert by nature, given the right atmosphere you could be really outgoing today.

• *Sunday 5 March* •

It's all about give and take today, and making compromises if necessary. This may not strike you as especially problematic, but be careful that you're not the one who's expected to do all the giving while someone else does all the taking. You may not even realize that everything seems to be operating on someone else's terms because you've got so used to it being this way. Decide what's fair and then redress the balance.

• *Monday 6 March* •

You could meet someone today who you're irresistibly at-tracted to. You may feel, however, very ambivalent about getting to know them better because something about them unsettles you. Let them make the first move and check them out thoroughly before you reach any decisions about taking your relationship further. Listening to what they say will give you some important clues.

• *Tuesday 7 March* •

You're in a strongly protective mood today and ready to leap to the defence of anyone you feel is being mistreated. Being aware of how other people are feeling creates tremendous empathy between you, and the contacts you make at this time will be warm and friendly. You may not be thinking logically, but your sensitivity will tell you what you need to know.

• *Wednesday 8 March* •

Your mind needs to be stimulated by new information and knowledge, and if there are any areas of interest you'd like to explore, this is an ideal time to do just that. Whether you sign up for a course or get some books out of the library, your intellectual curiosity is stimulated and the more you can discover about the world the better. You might even find an interest that will fascinate you for a long time to come.

• *Thursday 9 March* •

All matters related to work or your profession are going well today, and in your orderly state of mind you can tie up any loose ends that you never got around to before. Take advantage of this time, because you won't always feel so disciplined and manage to be this productive. You'll find it immensely rewarding to accomplish so much, so keep going while you're in such a methodical mood.

• *Friday 10 March* •

For reasons best known to yourself, you're inclined to keep your feelings and innermost thoughts private today. The only negative effect this might have is that by not letting others know how you feel, they can't offer the very support you need. This acts like a vicious circle and, unless you truly want to isolate yourself, it's up to you to break it. So take a deep breath and speak up!

• *Saturday 11 March* •

You're in a much more sociable mood today and you may even allow yourself to be persuaded to go to a party tonight. You've probably understood why you felt the need to shut everyone out for a while, and you can now put it behind you.

What may have surprised you is how your friends and loved ones accept you, no matter what. It's good to know.

• Sunday 12 March •

Several time-consuming projects are coming to a head at once and you may need to delegate if you don't want to be snowed under. You'll find that as long as you explain the situation and what you're up against, others will be only too happy to help. Whether these are domestic or professional issues, or both, rest assured that you will be able to manage them.

• Monday 13 March •

An event that takes place today totally changes your mind about something. You may meet someone who exerts a strong influence on you and makes you look at your life in a completely different way. Get a second opinion before you take any drastic action, because although your new point of view may be valid, it could just as easily trip you up.

• Tuesday 14 March •

If you're the sort of Virgo who doesn't normally throw caution to the winds, get ready to act out of character today. You're not in the mood for hard work and if you can take it easy and go at your own pace, you'll be more than happy. Even better, why not go out with a friend and treat yourselves to something you often talk about doing but never get round to? It will do you the world of good.

• Wednesday 15 March •

Your mental and emotional sides are completely in balance today and as a result you will find it easy to let someone know how much they mean to you. You're very articulate at the moment and know exactly which words to choose to express how you really feel. This paves the way for a much closer rapport with this person and a better understanding of each other.

• *Thursday 16 March* •

It would be very easy to be outspoken and to say exactly what you think today, but it would be wiser to weigh your words carefully first. You could be making assumptions based on the way you view the situation, without taking into consideration that other people may be seeing things differently. As a result, there could be a spat or argument, especially if people take umbrage at what you say. Proceed with caution!

• *Friday 17 March* •

Avoid making any decisive moves today, especially about matters involving your emotional life. If you allow your emotions to run amok, you may leap to the wrong conclusions and provoke an unnecessary crisis. If you do feel stirred up and have a bone to pick with someone, try to get a grip on your emotions before you say anything. Otherwise, all hell could break loose!

• *Saturday 18 March* •

A weekend away is just what the doctor ordered! Failing that, how about taking the day off? Preferably, you should go somewhere far away where you can totally relax and enjoy yourself. Not only will this make you feel recharged with energy, it might also help to revive a certain relationship. Giving yourself some time to have fun and relax will go a long way to restoring your flagging spirits.

• *Sunday 19 March* •

Are you slightly on edge today but don't know why? Don't worry, it's simply bottled-up tensions coming to the surface.

You might be tempted to take things out on the person you're closest to, but at least let them know how you're feeling so they don't think you're getting at them. Once you've let go of your irritability, you will feel much better and have some fun.

• *Monday 20 March* •

You may feel as if you're treading on eggshells today where a boss or authority figure is concerned. They're obviously not in the best of moods and you feel that it's your job to placate them. But can you do this? Arousing their anger would definitely not be in your best interests, and you may need to use a certain amount of tact and diplomacy just to keep things on an even keel.

• *Tuesday 21 March* •

This is a wonderful day for doing some entertaining or attending a social event. You're in a very generous and benevolent mood, and you feel the need to be in the company of those closest and dearest to you. You may also feel like splashing out, and if you decide to have a dinner party, you'll take great pleasure in choosing the menu and making everything look just right.

• *Wednesday 22 March* •

Someone is likely to surprise you today with an unexpected announcement. Whatever the news is, it will completely ambush you and, although you'll do your best to maintain a calm exterior, you won't be able to suppress your reaction entirely. This surprise may be positive or negative but, either way, you'll need to let it sink in for a while before taking further action.

• *Thursday 23 March* •

Your communications with others are very subjective today and coloured more by your feelings than anything else. You are really only interested in having deep and meaningful conversations with people, and anything less simply won't do. That may be all well and good when talking to a loved one, but other people may wonder why you're being so intense and tell you to lighten up. Use your Virgoan powers of discrimination.

• *Friday 24 March* •

If you've been putting up with a situation and have reached the end of your tether, you are now starting looking for a way to extricate yourself. You have a great desire for change and new experiences, but you may find yourself thwarted by circumstances beyond your control. You may not be able to sweep the board clean and start again overnight, but you can at least take a step in the right direction.

• *Saturday 25 March* •

You may decide to get involved in some kind of charitable activity today, such as working for the underprivileged. You want to feel that you can be of service in some way and give of yourself for the benefit of others. You may have a skill or ability that you can put to practical use and that would make all the difference to someone in need.

• *Sunday 26 March* •

You're very aware of the duties and obligations you have to live up to in relationships today, and you'll take them very seriously. Because of your strong need to give to others, this is more gratifying than challenging and you won't shirk from what's expected of you. You may act as a mentor for someone who looks up to you and respects what you think and say.

• Monday 27 March •

You feel more mentally alert today than you have in a while and you're eager to see and talk to people. The more energy you put into staying in touch with people, the better you'll feel. And you won't be the only one writing letters and picking up the phone because the chances are that all kinds of people you know will also take the initiative and get in touch. It promises to be a busy day!

• Tuesday 28 March •

If you have a problem or situation that you feel you can't handle on your own, this is a good time to discuss it with a sympathetic friend. You're probably spoilt for choice in that department, and you'll have to decide who could offer you the best viewpoint. There may be someone who often seeks out your advice and who'd be only too happy to reciprocate. You will feel much better once you've got things off your chest.

• Wednesday 29 March •

You may have to grapple with feelings of doubt today when something occurs which discourages you in some way. There's a lot you can do to improve this situation, provided you don't allow yourself to give up. You still have a few trump cards up your sleeve which you've yet to play, and with a little tact and patience you can still win the game. Before that happens, you may have to bide your time.

• Thursday 30 March •

Talk about a one-track mind! You may be preoccupied with a particular thought or idea that won't go away today, and you're in danger of getting totally wound up unless you find something to distract you. Whatever or whoever it is you're thinking about, it's crowding out all other thoughts and, no matter how hard you try, you can't seem to concentrate on anything else. Doing something physical may help.

• *Friday 31 March* •

You can learn so much about what makes you tick today, and particularly what motivates and inspires you. You may meet someone who acts as a catalyst in some way and who gives you the inspiration to do something you've never dared to think was possible. Whether this person becomes a friend or not is irrelevant – the purpose of meeting them is to help move you on.

APRIL AT A GLANCE

Love	♥ ♥ ♥
Money	£ $ £
Career	💻 💻
Health	☼ ☼

• *Saturday 1 April* •

If something breaks down or is in need of repair, this is a great day to see to it and get it out of the way. You have a feeling that things will only get worse if you leave them, and you don't want to put off until tomorrow what you can do today. In fact, you want to clear up any kind of unfinished business you might have so that you've got a clean slate. This will be very satisfying!

• Sunday 2 April •

Everything has to serve a practical purpose today and you're very focused on being as productive as possible. You get a natural high and a wonderful feeling of satisfaction from clearing up all the mess and putting everything in order. Anyone who comes into your orbit will be given a job to do and, given half the chance, you'd have the whole neighbourhood organized. You'll make a lot of progress.

• Monday 3 April •

Try to get as much physical activity as possible today and take advantage of your high energy levels. You're so full of beans that you can accomplish twice as much as normal and still keep going! Not only can you work hard but you can also play hard, so why not go out and have fun and show everyone just how much stamina you really have.

• Tuesday 4 April •

To say that your love life is hotting up today would be something of an understatement – an active volcano would be a better description. Passions are definitely ready to explode and your only problem is trying to keep some semblance of self-control. If you're a typical Virgo and pride yourself on staying calm, you may be in store for a big surprise over the coming fortnight when you discover just how intense your feelings can be.

• Wednesday 5 April •

You can decide which direction you want to go in today without having to compromise yourself in any way. No one is likely to accuse you of being selfish because it's obvious that you can have your own best interests at heart while still caring for those you love. As you now know, the happier you are, the more everyone around you will benefit.

• *Thursday 6 April* •

You'll thrive on meeting new people today and you'll handle any work-related social function with ease. Feeling so comfortable in yourself will enable you to mix with almost anyone without feeling nervous or shy. As for your private life, there might be an invitation to do something new. Even though you might have thought twice about it before, this time you'll jump at the idea.

• *Friday 7 April* •

On no account should you allow yourself to be undermined by someone who is apparently trying to make life difficult for you today. You've got so much going for you at the moment that it would be a shame to suffer a setback simply because this person's nose is out of joint. Perhaps the fact that you are going great guns is the reason for their sour grapes. Your best bet is to simply take no notice.

• *Saturday 8 April* •

Your curiosity is stimulated by someone you meet unexpectedly today. Although this person is a complete stranger, there's something tantalizingly familiar about them and you can't help wanting to find out more about them. There may be a simple explanation as to why you feel you've met before, or there may be a more mysterious reason. No wonder you're intrigued!

• *Sunday 9 April* •

You're feeling very strong-willed today and nobody has the slightest chance of changing your mind about anything. You've got a very specific idea of what you'd like to do now, and you know exactly who you want to spend the day with. Rarely have you been so determined to get your own way, or known more clearly what – or who – it is you want.

• Monday 10 April •

A huge piece of the jigsaw is falling into place and giving you the chance to see the bigger picture. You now have the foresight to make plans to expand your field of activities and to broaden the horizons of your life. However, before you do that you will have to pay attention to certain details. Thank goodness that is one of your strong suits!

• Tuesday 11 April •

You've got both the mental drive and the physical energy today to get moving. Whatever you embark on, your emotional conviction is so strong, and you feel so committed, that very little will deter you from your chosen path. It's the perfect opportunity to make progress at work or in an emotional matter. You may be acting more on instinct than any rational decision, but it all makes perfect sense to you.

• Wednesday 12 April •

You continue to follow your intuition today. This approach to life may be starting to alarm some people who are used to you adopting a more cautious attitude. It's almost as if you have an invisible radar system which tells you who you can trust and what is the right course of action to take. You can't expect everyone to go along with you so it's vitally important that you trust yourself.

• Thursday 13 April •

A certain someone has set your pulse racing and you could easily be carried away by the intensity of your emotions today. It's not everyday that you're ambushed by your feelings in this way, and it's rather disconcerting, to say the least, not to be able to analyse what's happening to you. For now, the best you can do is allow yourself to be swept along in the emotional current.

• *Friday 14 April* •

You need the security of your normal routine today to try to restore some order to your life. Following well-established patterns will bring you back to earth and help you begin to take stock of where you stand. You'll find that even the most mundane tasks are oddly comforting and reassuring now, because they give you the impression that you've regained some control over your life.

• *Saturday 15 April* •

You feel as if you're back in the driving seat today and you're quite happy to take things slowly for a while. Although you don't feel afraid of taking the initiative, you're quite curious to see if someone else will do all the running about. Any conversations you have will be direct and to the point, and if anyone tries to beat around the bush you'll have no hesitation in confronting them.

• *Sunday 16 April* •

Enjoy a day of leisure today without putting yourself under any pressure to do anything. You might feel like seeing some old friends and catching up on the gossip. The feedback you get from these chums could prove invaluable, especially if they help you to put recent events in perspective. You may not have all the answers, but at least you will have a few vital clues.

• *Monday 17 April* •

If you're true to your Sun sign you probably don't usually overindulge in food and drink, but given the social whirl today you might well be tempted! Whether it's business or pleasure, there are ample opportunities to be with fun and interesting people and you don't want to miss out. You might even make a few helpful connections for the future.

• *Tuesday 18 April* •

Whether it's a special day or not, don't be surprised if you receive a bunch of flowers or some other token of gratitude and admiration from someone. You make a good impression wherever you go today, and even people you don't normally get on with very well will seem to show you more warmth than usual. Could it be something to do with your own friendly attitude?

• *Wednesday 19 April* •

Above all else, be yourself today and you'll easily be able to stand your ground. Someone you know through your career may try to coerce you into agreeing to something that you have reservations about. They may have plenty of clout but, provided you don't allow yourself to be intimidated by them, they'll soon realize that they're wasting their time.

• *Thursday 20 April* •

Nobody is going to get away with pulling the wool over your eyes today. If a remark by a colleague or associate doesn't ring true, your suspicions will soon be raised. If you ignore these suspicions, you might kick yourself later on. Besides, you need to find out what this person is playing at. If they are making suggestions to you, don't commit yourself to anything until you know exactly what is involved.

• *Friday 21 April* •

Confident and self-assured is how you come across today. All your current hard work is paying dividends and everything is running smoothly and on schedule. Even if a problem does crop up, you're thinking so creatively that you'll come up with a solution in no time at all. You can gain valuable experience in your chosen field in the next few weeks.

• *Saturday 22 April* •

You and your partner may clash today over a difference of opinion that both of you feel strongly about. You're both so keen on sticking to your guns that you will either reach a stalemate or have a blazing row. Although you may normally be more accommodating in this sort of situation, on this occasion you're unwilling to compromise. Why does it matter so much to you?

• *Sunday 23 April* •

Ready for something completely different? You're in the mood for doing something out of the ordinary today, and the only way to manage that is to forget all about your normal activities and try something new. Even a brief respite from your Sunday routine will make you feel better. You're keen on anything that's fun, especially if it's also a little bit risky and it gets your adrenalin going. Go for it!

• *Monday 24 April* •

If someone challenges your ideas today, they'll actually be doing you a favour because they will help you to broaden your thinking. The insights they offer you about yourself will give you plenty of food for thought about how flexible you are when it comes to changing your mind. And the good news is that looking at yourself in a new way will allow you to communicate more freely and openly.

• Tuesday 25 April •

If you have an appreciation of art or music, this is a wonderful day to go to a concert or see an exhibition. You're in the mood to be inspired by something beautiful that takes you out of your everyday routine. This isn't a day to spend alone, and if there's someone who would love a cultural day out as much as you, take them with you. You'll have a whale of a time.

• Wednesday 26 April •

You need to find a balance today between taking your responsibilities to heart and staying open to exciting new possibilities. As long as you can have both structure and change, you can move forward and not get stuck in a rut. There's a momentum in your life now that is naturally discarding what's past its sell-by date and presenting you with fresh opportunities.

• Thursday 27 April •

You're feeling very restless today and you'll be much happier if you can get out and about. This is easier said than done and you may be forced to stay put or reach a compromise. The best way around this is to keep your mind occupied so you can counteract any boredom that threatens to set in. Once you're absorbed in something you'll feel happier and much more settled.

• Friday 28 April •

If you've been going at it hammer and tongs recently, your body might need a rest today to recover from all the stresses and strains. You can either just slow down a bit and not take on so much, or you could spoil yourself and give yourself a treat. Either way, make sure you nip your tiredness in the bud before it becomes full-blown exhaustion.

• *Saturday 29 April* •

If your expectations of a relationship are high, you won't be disappointed today. The love of your life comes up trumps and proves that they are everything you hoped they would be. This dispels any doubts you might have had about how reliable or committed they were. Now you can let down that emotional guard that you had so firmly in place.

• *Sunday 30 April* •

Your sensitivity to other people's moods and feelings today means you can strike up intimate conversations with those close to you. You may think you know someone inside out but they could reveal something about themselves that takes you totally by surprise. You'll probably be sworn to secrecy, but that's OK because it isn't your style to betray a confidence.

MAY AT A GLANCE

Love	♥ ♥ ♥
Money	£ $ £
Career	💻 💻 💻 💻 💻
Health	☼

• *Monday 1 May* •

You might have to jolt someone out of their lethargy today if you want to make the most of the day. It doesn't look as if they're going to provide you with the stimulating company you crave because they're probably more in the mood to take it easy. You may think if you can't beat them, join them – unless you decide to do your own thing.

• *Tuesday 2 May* •

The accent is on working relationships today and it seems that you can't take anything for granted where a certain person is concerned. They may be unreliable or not pulling their weight and this will have a direct effect on you. They won't like being confronted about their performance, but ignoring the problem would only make it worse so be prepared to speak up.

• *Wednesday 3 May* •

If there's any possibility of a misunderstanding today, that is probably exactly what will happen, unless you take great pains to double-check everything. Whatever you say could be misconstrued, so take every precaution necessary to ensure that your communications with others are clear. Stay on the ball because you're just as likely to get the wrong end of the stick as someone else.

• *Thursday 4 May* •

If you're feeling under the weather today, pace yourself as much as possible and don't force yourself to do more than you can manage. However, if you're a typical Virgo you have a strong sense of duty that might not let you off the hook so easily. It's important that you weigh up what really needs to be done today and what you can legitimately put off until tomorrow. What is the point of wearing yourself into the ground?

• *Friday 5 May* •

Talk about not seeing you for dust! You feel like a new person today and you're ready to tackle almost anything. The only cautionary note is that you're burning up a lot of nervous energy which can become stressful if you overdo it. You've got everything to play for and, professionally, you can get ahead by leaps and bounds. You'll be reaching the finishing line when everyone else has only just left the starting blocks. There's no stopping you now!

• *Saturday 6 May* •

Your romantic imagination catches fire today so you might fancy dropping some strong hints to a certain someone to book a candlelit table for two. You're in the mood to be wined and dined and anything more prosaic simply won't fit the bill. This idealism will make you expect a lot from other people but you could feel very disappointed when they fail to live up to your expectations.

• *Sunday 7 May* •

You feel at your best today, both physically and mentally, and you want to pack as much as you possibly can into your day. Your outlook is so positive that you feel you can really go for what you want with the complete optimism that you'll get it. Your lighthearted and expansive mood is bound to be infectious, and everyone will feel better simply from being in your company.

• *Monday 8 May* •

You'll spend a lot of your day in conversation with people that you share strong links and common aims with. Whether you're part of a large organization or simply a group of local residents, you're determined to make some changes and leave your mark. Some fantastic opportunities could come your way today, so make sure you spot them when they arrive!

• *Tuesday 9 May* •

You're going to be doing more talking than listening today because it's imperative that you get your point of view across.

Your mind is crystal clear and you can state your position in such a way that people will be sympathetic and receptive to what you're saying. Once you've announced your intentions and heard what others have to say, you can reach a better understanding.

• Wednesday 10 May •

You're very clear about your personal objectives today and feel motivated to accomplish any task that helps you achieve those aims. The only disadvantage to such dedication is that someone close to you could accuse you of being too wrapped up in yourself. It might help if you step back for a moment and see things from their angle, since there's no point in alienating anyone.

• Thursday 11 May •

You haven't got a lot of time for frivolity today because the demands of your everyday life leave little room for anything else. Although you're able to compartmentalize so that you can concentrate on whatever you need to be doing, another part of you is longing for a little more spontaneity in your life. Simply being aware of that will help you to make room for it.

• Friday 12 May •

Ready to let your hair down? You're rewarded for all your recent hard work by an invitation to somewhere special. The chances are that it's somewhere you've never been before, and just the thought of a new experience will fill you with delight and anticipation. This is the perfect opportunity to dress up and be a little more daring than usual.

• Saturday 13 May •

If you've been in dispute over something and it's been hanging over you, things may well come to a head today when you have no choice but to resolve the issue once and for all. Luckily, you're in an assertive mood and more than equipped to deal with the person concerned. If anything, you might overreact which won't help matters much. Keep your cool!

• *Sunday 14 May* •

You'll enjoy some very positive comments today from both friends and family. Having so much praise heaped on you will probably make you feel light-headed, and it may take you a while to float back down to earth. Although Virgos have a natural modesty, it won't do you any harm to take as much pride in your accomplishments as others do.

• *Monday 15 May* •

You're taken out of your usual surroundings today and, whether it's for business or pleasure, it looks as though you'll thoroughly enjoy yourself. This is especially likely if you can spend the day in excellent company, and an acquaintance could well turn into a friend as a result of the time you spend together. Be prepared for an unexpected but delightful treat.

• *Tuesday 16 May* •

If you've been wondering what to do for the best over a financial undertaking, you may decide to go ahead with it today. If you're a typical Virgo, it's not your style to take any unnecessary risks. This project almost seems too good to be true, but you've done your homework and everything appears to be above board. With your natural thoroughness, you're sure to have covered every eventuality.

• *Wednesday 17 May* •

You can't put your finger on why it is you have a sense of disquiet today. Everything may be fine in your outer life, but inside all is not well. It could be that you haven't acknowledged to yourself how you're really feeling, so all you're aware of is a vague sense of dissatisfaction. Try to get to the bottom of what's wrong, especially if you are covering up some deep-seated emotions. You can't mask your true feelings forever.

• Thursday 18 May •

The atmosphere could be rather tense today. If you feel on edge and your temper is about to fray, take a deep breath and decide if you really want to cause a row. Even with your self-discipline it may still be virtually impossible to keep things on an even keel, but at least you can embark on a damage limitation scheme and keep conflict to a minimum.

• Friday 19 May •

Your competitive streak comes to the fore today and you'll make sure you do your best to surpass yourself. Your mental alacrity is so good that you're likely to outsmart even the toughest competition, and while it isn't a good idea to be complacent, your chances of making your mark look extremely good. Rise to the occasion and you'll do yourself proud.

• Saturday 20 May •

You may have difficulty knowing where your allegiances lie today. On no account should you allow yourself to be manipulated by a relative who may be trying the 'divide and rule' strategy. Getting embroiled in a family feud would be a waste of time and energy and, although you may see both sides of the argument, it's not your battle to fight. However, a certain person may not agree with you, so take care.

• Sunday 21 May •

You need a change of air today and a break from your usual Sunday routine. This is especially likely if you spent yesterday walking around on eggshells. This is an ideal day to take up a new interest or put more time into an existing one. Not only will it add a new dimension to your life, it will also help you to unwind. You've got more talent than you give yourself credit for and it's just waiting to be used.

• Monday 22 May •

Every now and then you like to take an inventory of your life to see if you need to make any changes. What you may decide today is that you need greater job satisfaction, and one way to have that is to take on more responsibility. As long as you find the extra workload rewarding and worthwhile, you'll be more than happy with your lot.

• Tuesday 23 May •

You can enjoy your own company today or spend a pleasant time with friends and loved ones. In fact, you're feeling so easy-going and content that you don't mind whether you're sociable or not. You have plenty to occupy yourself if you do spend time on your own but, equally, you're more than happy to have a good natter with your favourite bunch of people.

• Wednesday 24 May •

You're feeling very single-minded today and not in the mood to waste time. You're leaving nothing to chance so you want to organize your day in such a way that you can get the most out of it. Maximum efficiency is what you're aiming for, and if anyone is dragging their feet you'll soon have them shaping up. It's your turn to call the shots so don't be afraid to ask for what you want.

• *Thursday 25 May* •

Matters of the heart are uppermost in your mind today. You feel very warm and trusting towards others and this could attract a potential partner if you're currently a solo Virgo. If you do meet someone new, you'll most likely fall head over heels in love with them. A relationship that starts today is a marriage made in heaven because you are so in tune with one another and you share similar aspirations.

• *Friday 26 May* •

Your rational side is fighting hard to gain control today and it looks as if it's going to be quite a battle! Head and heart are vying for supremacy and you're left feeling utterly confused about how to behave. Why not try combining your thoughts and feelings instead of thinking you've got to follow one or the other, and then you'll be in a much stronger position to decide what you want.

• *Saturday 27 May* •

This is an ideal day to escape from your usual routine and sort yourself out. Your thoughts are racing and you're probably a bundle of nerves, so what better solution than to get away from it all and have a rest. The worst thing you could do is sit around endlessly turning things over in your mind, because you'll only end up going round in circles. If you're trying to reach a solution, simply let yourself unwind and the answers will come.

• *Sunday 28 May* •

Some marvellous opportunities come your way today, and they'll enable you to combine your habitual sense of caution with a strong streak of optimism. You won't want to throw yourself into anything without thinking it through first, yet you could miss out on something wonderful if you drag your feet for too long. Maybe it's time to take a calculated risk or a leap of faith, and to trust that everything will work out well?

• *Monday 29 May* •

Although you may not get a lot done at work or when tackling finances today, on an inner level you're incredibly busy getting to grips with patterns of behaviour that you recognize in yourself. Some are positive and some are negative, and the fact that you know the difference is half the battle. An old maxim says that knowledge is power, and you will certainly feel stronger if you can be honest in getting to know yourself better.

• *Tuesday 30 May* •

After yesterday's soul-searching, you're ready to increase the tempo of your social life and get out and meet friends. You're in the mood to talk to kindred spirits and share your new discoveries with them over the next few weeks. However, you probably won't want to spend the whole time in deep conversation as you've got something else on the agenda – having fun!

• *Wednesday 31 May* •

Getting used to the new you? An inner decision that you've made is already beginning to show in your outer life and people are beginning to notice something different about you. This could be as simple as a change of attitude, but the repercussions are far greater and more positive than you could have ever anticipated, as the coming weeks will prove. You've got a lot to look forward to!

JUNE AT A GLANCE

Love	♥ ♥
Money	£
Career	💻 💻 💻 💻 💻
Health	☼

• *Thursday 1 June* •

You're definitely not backwards in coming forwards today. Someone who may have underestimated you in the past is taken aback by how resolute you are, especially where your personal goals are concerned. You see this as a matter of integrity, and if that means standing up for yourself and facing the music whatever the consequences, you're prepared to do it.

• *Friday 2 June* •

Today's New Moon in the career portion of your chart heralds a new phase in which you may feel you need to redefine your aims and aspirations. There is so much working in your favour, particularly now that you have the confidence to sell yourself. You really are your own best PR person at the moment – who better than you knows what skills you have and what an asset you are?

• *Saturday 3 June* •

There's a tug of war going on today between the demands of your family and your career. Perhaps you long to spend time at home but instead you've got to finish off some important work. A loved one's patience is wearing thin, and they probably won't be very sympathetic if they know you have other priorities as well as them this weekend. You'll have to do some serious sucking up if you don't want to be *persona non grata*.

• *Sunday 4 June* •

Think about something you'd really like to do today and then see if you can make it happen. There's more within your reach than you think, and it just takes a little bit of imagination to discover what's possible. As long as you don't fall into the trap of limiting your thinking and setting a limit on what might be, anything could happen now. So think big!

• *Monday 5 June* •

You may have to be slightly selfish today in order to achieve what you set out to do. It's very easy to get side-tracked by other people's considerations and, although that may be inevitable at times, you really must focus on what you need now and not waiver from the task. You can expect more support than you'd thought possible, which only goes to prove that you're doing the right thing.

• *Tuesday 6 June* •

You'll probably feel secretly pleased with yourself today but you're not about to blow your own trumpet. You'd much rather quietly give yourself the credit you're due and keep everything low-key. Fanfares and red carpets are not your style, but provided that you – and the people who matter – know that you've done a good job, that's reward enough. It will be easy to get on well with someone who's older or wiser than you.

• *Wednesday 7 June* •

You'll take great pleasure in working behind the scenes today, especially if that involves doing something creative. Even if you're working on your own, you're so absorbed in what you're doing that you would barely be aware of anyone else's presence anyway. Being mentally engaged in this way is your favourite way to work and gives you a great sense of fulfilment.

• *Thursday 8 June* •

The spotlight is on close relationships today and you may have to contend with some unwanted feelings. You could be at a crucial turning point in an emotional matter, and the pivotal issue is the extent to which you can be honest with yourself about this. It's not always easy to face up to certain truths, but if you can manage this a certain person will be willing to forgive and forget.

• *Friday 9 June* •

A burst of inspiration is what is needed to get you through the day. It's not that you're short of ideas, it's simply that none of them sets you alight. It's one of those days when you feel fraught or dissatisfied. The harder you work at something, the less you feel you have achieved. As a result you need to do something to get you through this block. Go for a walk or do something that will get your creative juices flowing again.

• *Saturday 10 June* •

You may feel that you're not entirely in charge of your finances today, so you're looking for ways to regain control of the purse strings. If you're a true-to-type Virgo, it won't take you long to come up with a solution. Your well-known attention to detail means that you will soon see where you've slipped up so you can put things right in no time.

• *Sunday 11 June* •

You feel very innovative today. You are thinking in a very fresh and original way, so new solutions to old problems will simply pop into your head. In fact, you'll wonder how you ever got so stuck in an old dilemma when you discover how easy it is to extricate yourself from it. And now that it's no longer a thorn in your side, you can focus with renewed clarity on the days and weeks ahead.

• *Monday 12 June* •

You feel free to pursue your goals wholeheartedly today, whether these are professional or personal. Everything suddenly seems within reach and the pieces are falling into place. Friends and colleagues are supportive and they will offer whatever help you need. What's more, you have a wonderfully warm and reassuring feeling that everything will work out for the best.

• *Tuesday 13 June* •

It seems that you need to smooth over a few ruffled feathers today, but you're more than happy to accommodate a certain person's feelings. You have a sneaking suspicion that this isn't a serious fit of pique so much as a demand for some attention. In no time at all you'll be able to cajole this person into a better mood, and then harmony will be restored.

• *Wednesday 14 June* •

Someone may try to use their powers of persuasion to convince you about something you're in two minds about today. Fortunately you're not in the mood to be easily swayed, and you're determined to show that you too can be a force to be reckoned with. It looks as though this person seriously underestimated you if they thought you'd be a pushover. You can obviously look after yourself!

• *Thursday 15 June* •

A personal matter concerning a family member demands your attention today and leaves very little time for anything else.

There's more to this particular problem than meets the eye, so don't make any assumptions or have any preconceived ideas about how to handle the situation. Keep an open mind and then you'll soon root out the cause of the upset once you've started talking.

● *Friday 16 June* ●

Your recent decision to inject new zest into areas of your life that had gone stale is showing results in all sorts of ways. You're finding more time to do what you want to do, and because you're less at the beck and call of others, you are able to live your life more on your terms. Do something that will allow you to shine today because there will be a very special opportunity for you to be noticed.

● *Saturday 17 June* ●

Talk about having ants in your pants! You're so eager to get out and about today that, unless they're quick, nobody will be able to catch up with you. You might actually prefer to spend the day on your own, so you are able to go at your own pace and do as you please. Life's too short to waste, and you're anxious to pack as much into the day as you possibly can.

● *Sunday 18 June* ●

You're more home-based today than you were yesterday, and if you have children, they're likely to take up most of your time. Over the next few weeks you will find that friends play an increased role in your life. You could spend more time than usual with some of your favourite people. You will also enjoy meeting some like-minded people through a club or society.

• *Monday 19 June* •

Need to calm your nerves? You're quite happy to have a quiet and uneventful day today because that's exactly what you're in the mood for. Taking refuge in your work is one way of finding a peaceful haven – provided you can keep the rest of the world at bay. If that's too tall an order, make a point of not taking any more work on than you have to. Relax by doing something enjoyable.

• *Tuesday 20 June* •

Someone you met through a professional connection and took an instant liking to is giving you some very strong signals today. You might choose to play it cool and not give them any indication of how keen you really are on them. Alternatively, you might go for broke and give them the encouragement they need to ask you out. Take care when tackling any detailed work because your mind may keep drifting off to other things.

• *Wednesday 21 June* •

If you've taken yourself in hand recently and generally feel much more fit and healthy as a result, you could get a chance to put that to the test today. The upshot may well be that although you're definitely in better condition than you were, there is still room for improvement! It could be a simple case of needing to take a little more exercise, provided you don't make it hard work.

• *Thursday 22 June* •

You're walking on air today because a little bird has told you that you're about to receive some professional recognition or a big pat on the back. This could be a promotion, a rise in salary or even public acclaim. Now that the news has leaked out, it's hard for you to carry on as normal. What's agonizing is that you have no idea when you're going to be told in person. Patience!

• *Friday 23 June* •

Simply go with the flow today and try not to impose your agenda on anything or anyone. There's a lot happening behind the scenes and it's driving you mad not knowing what's going on. Trying to analyse the situation won't help either because you don't have the full facts at the moment so you can't make a rational assessment. Use your Virgoan self-discipline to think about something else until you know more about what's going on.

• *Saturday 24 June* •

You're in a very constructive mood today and you want to do as much as you can on a very practical level. This is an ideal time to complete those repairs that you didn't manage to finish before. You might even want to do some gardening or decorating. You'll find doing lots of physical work is very therapeutic and a good antidote to all the mental stress that you've had to put up with lately.

• *Sunday 25 June* •

The more you do today the better you feel. You gain tremendous satisfaction from even the most insignificant job, especially when you see what a difference it makes when you've finished. Although you'll eventually run out of steam and have to stop, you're determined to keep going in the meantime. This may also help you to work off some irritation caused by a friend or close partner.

• *Monday 26 June* •

You're ready to experience life without a safety net today. You may well feel that you're capable of achieving so much more than you are at the moment, and you're now willing to go out on a limb to prove it. Whatever strategy you use to demonstrate your talents and abilities, it's bound to be a departure from your old style, and that's what will ultimately make the difference. So be brave and prepared to try something new.

• Tuesday 27 June •

Your head feels a little woolly today and as a result there's a danger of misunderstandings or lack of communication. It's almost as if your mind has gone into soft focus, and so it's difficult to stay on the ball. It would be better to defer any discussions or decisions until you can come out of your reverie and you've got your feet firmly back on the ground. In the meantime, creative and imaginative projects will go well.

• Wednesday 28 June •

You might feel somewhat lacklustre today and have to force yourself to do even the simplest thing. You just can't summon up the energy. The more straightforward and routine your agenda is, the more lethargic you will feel. You'd far rather have a more eventful day than a predictable one. Inject a little excitement into your day, otherwise you could soon lose patience or do something deliberately designed to make the fur fly.

• Thursday 29 June •

The caring side of your nature is to the fore today, especially if you have a cause that you believe in. You're not so much concerned with individuals but more with a group of people that need help. If you belong to an organization that is actively involved with trying to make people's lives better, you'll want to dedicate as much of your time as possible to them.

• *Friday 30 June* •

You are working like mad today to try to get a backlog of work finished before the weekend. Fortunately, your determination is supplying all the energy you need to get things done, so you won't have to spend all weekend recovering from the effort you expend today. Spare a little time to start thinking about ways to spread your wings in your career or public life. Some great opportunities will soon be on their way to you!

JULY AT A GLANCE

Love	♥ ♥
Money	£
Career	💻 💻 💻
Health	☼

• *Saturday 1 July* •

You feel years younger than you really are today and ready to burn the candle at both ends. You don't want to waste a single minute of this renewed energy, and while others may be quite happy to contemplate their navels, you want action. You'll seize the initiative at the drop of a hat, and if you can do something that puts you in charge you'll quickly rise to the occasion.

• *Sunday 2 July* •

Even if you were out on the tiles last night, you're still bright-eyed and bushy-tailed this morning and keen to plan how to spend the day. Although you're not feeling quite so energetic as yesterday, you still feel amazingly full of life. A loved one or partner is feeling very lovey-dovey today, and they're keeping their fingers crossed that you'll respond in kind.

• *Monday 3 July* •

After being in such a lively mood all weekend, you may fancy having a more low-key day when you don't have to do anything very strenuous. Your imagination is stimulated and you're in the mood to write or do some other creative activity. You'll be in your element if your work has an artistic slant to it. A member of the family could have a powerful impact on you – and won't they know it!

• *Tuesday 4 July* •

Someone at work is ready to fly off the handle and it looks as if you're right in the firing line. It's not so much a personal issue but more a case of them wanting to offload their frustrations and you happening to be a convenient scapegoat. Try to find a way to defuse the situation because you really don't want to create an even bigger scene by losing your cool.

• *Wednesday 5 July* •

Hold on tight! It's one of those roller-coaster days when you feel you have no control whatsoever over what happens. All you can do is take a deep breath and let things take their natural course. Just when you think you're heading one way, there'll be a sudden and dramatic change of direction. Although this may be a daunting prospect, part of you is secretly excited by it all. At least you can't say life is boring!

• *Thursday 6 July* •

Even though you can take life at a more leisurely pace today, you've still got a lot on your mind that you need to attend to. You are very wrapped up in your emotions now, and you may be looking for an excuse to tell someone how much you care about them. Talking to a good friend about your predicament will give you a clearer perspective on what your next move should be.

• *Friday 7 July* •

If you're going away soon, your thoughts are probably already centred on what to take and whether you need to add anything to your holiday shopping list. Whether your bank balance is in a healthy state or not, you feel like treating yourself to something special. Even if you aren't going on holiday, you still fancy buying yourself a little luxury. Indulging yourself will do wonders for you now.

• *Saturday 8 July* •

Is it a case of absence makes the heart grow fonder or out of sight out of mind? If you get the opportunity to have some time on your own this weekend, it might surprise you to discover that things won't go the way you expected. Your feelings about a certain person could give you food for thought. This will give you a chance to rethink a relationship, decide how you feel about it and see if there are any changes you want to make.

• *Sunday 9 July* •

If you come to the conclusion that you need to restructure a fundamental aspect of your life, you'll feel impatient to set it in motion and talk it over with whoever else is involved. Taking time out to reflect on your needs has led you to ask yourself whether your natural inclination to devote yourself to others is compromising your well-being. Perhaps it's time to be a little bit selfish?

• *Monday 10 July* •

You're ready to defend something that you strongly believe in and feel passionate about. Your emotions are stirred up and you are able to express yourself with great conviction and intensity today. The impact that you have on others will be considerable and, because what you say rings true, they'll be more receptive and open to the ideas you want to put to them. They may even change their minds about something.

• *Tuesday 11 July* •

Your integrity alone wins people over today, and whatever it is that you're involved in draws a lot of support. Rest assured that you have the respect and admiration of those you count on to help you make a difference. You're on a mission to change a situation for the better, and now that you're part of a team, you feel quietly confident that you've got what it takes.

• *Wednesday 12 July* •

Your campaign to improve the status quo is still very much in your thoughts, and today your thoughts turn to some home improvements. If you want to create more space at home, perhaps you could move around the furniture or come up some other space-saving ideas. You've probably felt cramped for a while, but it's only now that you're sufficiently fired up to make any significant changes.

• *Thursday 13 July* •

You could have an unexpected visitor today and they might hang around longer than you anticipate. Whereas you might have found this very disruptive before, this time you're more than happy to have them around. You'll soon find that your normal routine goes out of the window when you realize what fun they are and how much you enjoy their stimulating company.

• *Friday 14 July* •

You've got a lot on your plate today, but at least you can delegate and not have to carry everything on your shoulders.

Your systematic approach to getting the job done stands you in good stead and gives you the head start you need. Luckily, you have plenty of stamina at the moment and your mental energy alone will keep you on top of things.

• *Saturday 15 July* •

Thinking of doing some entertaining? You're in exactly the right mood, so how about rustling up a last-minute guest-list if you don't have anything else planned? It's a good idea to mix friends and colleagues because they could hit it off really well. Alternatively, perhaps you would prefer to go out on the tiles with some chums. Whatever you do today looks like being a lot of fun, so enjoy yourself!

• *Sunday 16 July* •

Someone could be forgiven for thinking you'd taken a vow of silence today. It's not that you're feeling particularly antisocial, it's just that you've done a lot of talking recently and you now feel like some peace and quiet. What most appeals to you is spending a low-key day with people who don't expect you to make an effort with them. Once you've recharged your batteries, you might feel like doing a few things around the house.

• *Monday 17 July* •

Trust your instincts today, even if they're telling you something that your more rational side finds hard to believe. You're finding it a struggle to trust what someone is telling you, despite the fact that what they're saying seems perfectly acceptable on the surface. Your suspicions are aroused, and that's a sure sign that you have to tread very carefully where this person is concerned.

• *Tuesday 18 July* •

It's another day when it's hard to separate fact from fiction, and it's still not clear whether someone is genuine or not. Getting to the bottom of whether you're deluding yourself or you're the one who's being duped is no mean feat. Rely on your intuition, but back it up with your ability to discriminate, and then you should come up with your answer. If in doubt, bide your time.

• *Wednesday 19 July* •

Your confidence could take a knock today and make you question something you've invested so much of yourself in. You'll probably need to go away and think about the implications of such a loss of faith and whether you want to continue as before. Don't make any hasty decisions, because things may seem much more bleak than they really are. Everything could be as right as rain again in a few days.

• *Thursday 20 July* •

You may be looking at things in very black-and-white terms today, when in fact you need to take every shade of grey into consideration. It's easy to be inflexible when you feel angry or disappointed, but you'll only be hard on yourself if you take too rigid a stance. Perhaps a partner is testing your patience or you feel that a situation is getting out of hand. Taking responsibility for your part in what has happened is the quickest way to release yourself from this situation.

• *Friday 21 July* •

A close relationship comes up trumps today and you will really appreciate what this person means to you and how you can count on them. You realize that a certain someone will support you through thick and thin, and this restores your trust in human nature. You were probably beginning to wonder if you'd misplaced it somewhere along the way, but now you know beyond a shadow of a doubt that all is well.

• Saturday 22 July •

Your actions speak louder than words today and leave no one in any doubt that you mean business. A show of strength on your part gives you the authority you need if a family member is going to respect and look up to you. Although it's probably not your style to be heavy-handed, when the situation demands it you can show you've got teeth.

• Sunday 23 July •

The time has come to put your cards on the table and show a certain someone exactly how you feel. This is especially important if you want your relationship to improve. There's no point in holding yourself back because it's obvious to both of you how you feel. Once you've lowered your guard, you can enjoy a closeness and intimacy that will make you question why you were so cagey up until now.

• Monday 24 July •

Even if you tried to be sensible today you would never manage it. Your heart is totally in control of your head and it's issuing instructions left, right and centre! Your feelings tell you that everything you're thinking and doing makes total sense, so there is no way you can maintain a rational outlook. This is especially likely if a certain person has swept you off your feet. It's called falling in love!

• Tuesday 25 July •

Your charisma opens many doors for you today, so make the most of it! You radiate charm and confidence, and if that sparkle in your eye gets any brighter, you're likely to set fire to something! It's just as well that your innate Virgoan modesty will prevent you from getting too carried away. Even so, you'll enjoy flirting with someone or charming them into submission.

• *Wednesday 26 July* •

You can sense what people are going to say before they've even said it today, and you'll start to wonder if you're a mindreader. The fact is that your sensitivity is heightened and you can pick up feelings and moods more easily than usual. This will help you to tune into the people around you. A personal relationship will benefit enormously from this awareness and help you to feel closer than ever.

• *Thursday 27 July* •

You're feeling ultra-convivial today, and the more you can get out and about the better. A reunion with a favourite group of old friends is an ideal way to while away a few hours. You're likely to be the centre of attention because of your chatty personality, and everyone will be hanging on every word you have to say. Be prepared for lots of ooohs and aaahs!

• *Friday 28 July* •

If someone accuses you of acting out of character today, it could be because they simply don't know you very well. Thinking that they had you taped was an error of judgement on their part, and you may need to educate them about the complexity of human nature. Showing your true colours may have left them speechless, but at least they now know the real you.

• Saturday 29 July •

It looks as though you'll be up to your ears in domesticity today and you'll be kept extremely busy. Thank goodness you're prepared for any eventuality and have done as much of the groundwork as possible. Whether you're working on the house or the garden, you're tackling this particular project like a military campaign. Maximum efficiency yields maximum results. Other people will be very impressed with your efforts!

• Sunday 30 July •

If you're recovering from yesterday's exertions, you might decide to give yourself a well-earned rest today. You may still be tempted to add a few finishing touches to your handiwork, but the thought of a more sensual day enjoying good food and wine holds the greatest appeal. If you can invite a few friends round to share it with you, then so much the better.

• Monday 31 July •

You're back to your old industrious self today and ready to use your power and influence to set the ball rolling. You're in the perfect position to call the shots where a business associate or authority figure is concerned. Today's New Moon also signals that it's time to face up to certain fears or worries that have been dogging your footsteps recently. Get them out into the open, where you can deal with them once and for all.

AUGUST AT A GLANCE

Love	♥ ♥ ♥ ♥ ♥
Money	£ $
Career	💻 💻
Health	☼ ☼ ☼ ☼ ☼

• *Tuesday 1 August* •

You start the month feeling on top form and geared up for anything. In fact, you're so supercharged with energy that you'll make things happen with very little effort on your part. You know exactly where to channel your energies and, because your powers of concentration are much stronger than usual today, you can finish early and have time to relax and let off steam. What a satisfying day!

• *Wednesday 2 August* •

The power of positive thinking will work wonders for you today and it might even completely change the outcome of a potentially sticky situation. Things may look worse than they seem, but rather than imagine the worst thing that could possibly happen, look on the bright side and trust in that silver lining. Apart from anything else, it'll make it a lot easier to function in the meantime.

• *Thursday 3 August* •

Good news if you are currently single! Matters of the heart take a turn for the better today, and if you've tried every trick in the book to get someone's attention without success, you could strike lucky now. And about time, too! The lengths you've gone to make an impression may not have been wasted after all, and at last it seems that your amorous intentions are falling on fertile soil.

• Friday 4 August •

If you want to make the best of today you'll need make sure that you're in the limelight. Holding yourself back out of shyness or insecurity will mean missing a wonderful opportunity to get to know someone better. Your knees may be trembling and your heart thumping, but this could be your last chance to seize the moment. Go on, what have you got to lose?

• Saturday 5 August •

Proceed with caution where finances are concerned today. If you're about to hand over some money, think twice first because someone may be trying to pull a fast one on you or they may not have given you all the facts. It's not that you like to view other people with suspicion, but there are occasions when it's better to be safe than sorry. Read the small print on everything and be prepared to ask some awkward questions!

• Sunday 6 August •

Are you rushed off your feet? It's not surprising with the amount you've got on your plate. If you're packing for a holiday or long journey, make sure that you give yourself plenty of time because if you leave things to the last minute you're bound to forget something. If you're going out for the day, double-check the route or you could end up going in the wrong direction.

• Monday 7 August •

Life is full of excitement today and the more you can play things by ear the better. It's one of those days when you need to cast caution to the winds and live a little! You exude confidence and enthusiasm and your powers of attraction are at their strongest. Your love life is about to be spiced up, and with your libido chomping at the bit, a certain someone is bound to be mesmerized by your seductive charms.

• *Tuesday 8 August* •

You're in an outspoken mood today so, unless you watch what you say, you might put your foot in it. You'll need to temper your desire to be frank with an awareness of the other person's feelings. It won't be that easy to make amends if you say something you regret, and it could even drive a wedge between you and the person you least want to hurt. So try to think before you speak!

• *Wednesday 9 August* •

If you succeeded in curbing your tongue yesterday but didn't manage to get anything off your chest, you may be left with the uncomfortable feeling of bottling something up. Saying your piece doesn't have to be as difficult as you think, and you may be overestimating the impact of what you have to say. With a little tact and sensitivity you'll find the right words. Good luck!

• *Thursday 10 August* •

You'll need to find some space for yourself today, otherwise things will get too much for you. You're buzzing with all sorts of new ideas, but with the mayhem going on around you it's impossible to think straight. Once you're removed yourself from the fray, some of those ideas will start to germinate and, before you know it, you'll have a full-blown plan. Sharing it with a friend will help you to think things through.

• *Friday 11 August* •

Taking a trip down memory lane? You're happy to stick with what's familiar today, especially where friends and places are concerned. You don't want to wander too far afield and you'll take comfort in being with people that you share a long history with. Going out to a favourite restaurant or reminiscing about the past will evoke lots of wonderful memories. You might create a few new memories, as well!

● *Saturday 12 August* ●

You'll have to watch your critical side today because it will be very easy to find fault with everything someone says. Let's face it, nobody likes to have a barrage of criticism heaped on them, especially when they don't feel that it's justified. By all means point something out if you feel it's really important, but say it in the most constructive way you can find. Otherwise, there will be a very nasty atmosphere.

● *Sunday 13 August* ●

You've got a real spring in your step today, and the more you can feel free to do your own thing the better. You're in the mood to widen your horizons and break new ground, and if you can take off and explore new places, so much the better. If that's not an option, do something that will offer you a challenge or give you a sense of adventure. You might also meet someone who gives you plenty of food for thought.

● *Monday 14 August* ●

Is it time to move on to pastures new? You'll need to think long and hard today about a certain relationship and how well it's working. If you feel that it's lacking in some way and there's room for improvement, talk about your concerns and see if you can come up with a solution together. If in your heart you feel your liaison is beyond repair, have the courage to say so.

• *Tuesday 15 August* •

Are you ready to realize that burning ambition? If something has been holding you back recently, you'll be glad to know that today's Full Moon is giving you the green light to forge full steam ahead. You've got many different irons in the fire and, now that you're raring to go, there's nothing to stop you from reaching your goals. You have both the dedication and the determination, so watch out world!

• *Wednesday 16 August* •

You could either be tense and nervous or excited and restless today, depending on how you feel about the changes that are in the air. It may even be a combination of all of these emotions. No matter how you feel today, you know in your heart that it's time to shed an outworn skin and leave an aspect of the past behind. You no longer think of yourself in the same way that you once did or fit into the old mould. It's time for the birth of a new you!

• *Thursday 17 August* •

It would be an understatement to say that you're raring to go – you're about to break the speed of light and make history! A whole new side of you has been activated and it's giving you massive amounts of energy and motivation. You're in no doubt about what you want to do with your new-found dynamism, and there's no time like the present to get started.

• *Friday 18 August* •

Be careful of being overly single-minded today, otherwise your thinking could become too rigid. Although it's important that you maintain your focus, don't narrow it down to such a point that you block out the rest of the picture. To sustain your vision and make it concrete, it's imperative that you don't become fragmented, otherwise you'll end up not being able to see the wood for the trees.

• *Saturday 19 August* •

If there's a tug of war raging in you today about whether to go off gallivanting or stay at home and tackle the chores, it looks as though the domestic demands will win the battle. Much as you would love to indulge your frivolous side, you might as well reconcile yourself to the fact that you won't rest easy until you've got all those chores out of the way. There'll be plenty of time to play after that.

• *Sunday 20 August* •

You'll need some time today to consider how much progress you're making in your professional life. You know where you're heading, and you've probably calculated all the moves that will get you there, so it's simply a question of evaluating where you are now. This will be a much quicker process if you choose someone who knows you well to act as a sounding board.

• *Monday 21 August* •

You're very affected by somebody's mood today and you're so identified with their feelings that it will be hard to know where they end and you start. This will be distracting, to say the least, and it will make it virtually impossible for you to function normally. The only thing for it is to explain about the empathy you feel towards them and see what they say. Easier said than done if it's someone you hardly know.

• *Tuesday 22 August* •

Why are you being so defensive today? For some reason you feel under attack by a colleague or superior at work. Perhaps they are quick to criticize or you feel they are looking down their nose at you. If you step out from behind your guard for a moment, you could discover that things are not as personal as you imagined. Or are you getting a dose of your own medicine and having something pointed out to you that isn't up to scratch?

• Wednesday 23 August •

You can count your blessings today because someone who believes in you one hundred per cent is fighting your corner and putting in a good word for you. The timing is perfect – just as life was beginning to feel like an uphill struggle, it's now looking more like a leisurely downhill cruise! It's not quite time to rest on your laurels, though, but at least you can count not only on practical help but emotional support as well.

• Thursday 24 August •

Good fortune shines on all your endeavours today and gives you the chance to excel. You're being even more conscientious than usual, and you may even put in extra hours in order to prepare a suitable showcase for your talents. Coming second best is not an option right now, and although others may think that you're expecting too much of yourself, you refuse to sell yourself short. Keep up your high standards!

• Friday 25 August •

You have a flair for the dramatic today but be careful not to get carried away and end up making mountains out of molehills. Are you harbouring a resentment towards someone and trying to provoke them? It's better to come out with it and say exactly how you feel, because if you stir up an argument without saying what has caused it, it could backfire on you in a big way.

• *Saturday 26 August* •

A social occasion will give you the perfect opportunity today to spend time with a loved one in a relaxed and informal atmosphere. Life has been very hectic recently and you need to re-establish your relationship and enjoy one another's company. It would do you the world of good to let your hair down and dance the night away – or at least until your feet are screaming for a truce.

• *Sunday 27 August* •

Teamwork is the name of the game today and, provided the spirit of harmony and cooperation prevails, you'll get on famously with whoever happens to be around. It's a marvellous opportunity to organize a group outing, especially if you're doing something sociable. Start as you mean to go on by deciding what each person's role is going to be. If you end up with too many chiefs and not enough Indians, the furthest you'll get without someone throwing a tantrum will be the end of your road!

• *Monday 28 August* •

Have the tissues handy because someone may need a shoulder to cry on today. Although you'll feel sympathetic, it's worth asking yourself how much this particular person wants to help themselves and how much they are relying on other people to bail them out. It could be that they want to offload all their problems on to you, without taking any responsibility for them.

• *Tuesday 29 August* •

Even your best-laid plans could go up in smoke today, but don't panic. Provided you can come up with an alternative idea, things could turn out even better than you'd expected.

Someone keeps changing the goalposts and, as infuriating as that is, it does keep you on your toes and make you think on your feet. The best and most original creative solutions often occur in the midst of such confusion.

• *Wednesday 30 August* •

You could come up with a brainwave today that will transform the way you've been approaching a particular problem. Simply by seeing something from another angle can change the whole picture, and you're so excited about this new perspective that you can't wait to discuss it with someone. Make sure you choose a person who can appreciate your stroke of genius and who is as far-sighted as you.

• *Thursday 31 August* •

Don't count your chickens before they've hatched! Something that you thought was in the bag may prove to be more elusive than you imagined, and you can't help but feel disappointed. Try to take it in your stride and see whether you can turn things around. If you feel that the dice are loaded against you, maybe the whole thing was never meant to happen in the first place. You may have to put it down to experience.

SEPTEMBER AT A GLANCE

Love	♥ ♥ ♥ ♥ ♥
Money	£ $ £ $ £
Career	💻 💻
Health	☼ ☼ ☼ ☼ ☼

• *Friday 1 September* •

If someone at work or at home doesn't pull their weight today you'll be down on them like a ton of bricks. You need to work together as a partnership, and you can't afford to carry any passengers if you want to move forward together. Could it be that they no longer have the commitment but haven't admitted it to themselves? Brace yourself for a much-needed showdown.

• *Saturday 2 September* •

If you're a typical Virgo you'll be in your element today because your cool, rational approach is needed to solve a personal problem. You're able to go to the heart of the matter and dispel any emotional confusion that exists between you and a loved one. Once you've been able to clarify the situation, you can discuss how you both feel in a less heated way. This will help you to see the way forward.

• *Sunday 3 September* •

Take a good look at your finances today and see if there's any way you can increase your income or earn more interest on your savings. The more creatively you think about this, the more solutions you'll come up with. If the money's been rolling in recently, there's even more incentive to make a good investment and secure yourself a nice little nest-egg for the future. It may not be very exciting but it is good sense!

• *Monday 4 September* •

Feeling under par? Try not to take on too much today because you don't have as much energy as usual. It's more of a superficial tiredness than chronic fatigue, but if you overdo it you could become prone to picking up a cold or some other minor infection because your resistance is low. It will also help if you keep well away from anyone who is coughing or sneezing, and who generously wants to spread their germs in your direction.

• *Tuesday 5 September* •

If your schedule for today is looking boringly predictable, you'll be eager to do something different in order to break the routine. If you can find a way of building something fun into your day, you'll be more tolerant of anything tedious that you have to do. A change of scene will do you the world of good so try and get out and about, especially if you feel your patience wearing thin.

• *Wednesday 6 September* •

You're absorbed in an exciting new possibility today and you need to discuss how viable it is with someone who thinks along the same lines as you. Don't make the mistake of talking to anyone who is likely to dismiss your idea out of hand, because your enthusiasm could easily be crushed by their dismissive attitude. If this plan is to become reality, you need all the support you can get.

• *Thursday 7 September* •

Are you ready to take the plunge? Don't allow a fear of failure to hold you back today because you're so close to bringing a project or plan to fruition that it would be a shame to slam the brakes on now. Putting the finishing touches to this plan may involve sticking your neck out or swimming against the tide, but you've come too far now to change your mind. Have the courage of your own convictions!

• *Friday 8 September* •

You can get your way today without coming on too strong. This will stand you in good stead in a number of ways. For instance, if you've been wanting to buy something for your home this would be a great day to snap up a bargain. You might even haggle over the price or negotiate a discount simply by using your charm alone – and a little cheek!

• *Saturday 9 September* •

Keep the channels of communication wide open between you and a loved one today, and be prepared to talk out any differences of opinion between you. You may have been turning a blind eye to something that you can no longer ignore, and things could turn nasty unless you do something about it. Pretending that everything is all right when it's not can create a lot of unconscious anger.

• *Sunday 10 September* •

If you look back on what happened yesterday you'll realize that you learned a valuable lesson about being true to yourself. This gives you a wonderful feeling of authenticity, and your whole outlook is more positive and optimistic as a result. It's as if you've lanced a boil so that some healing can take place. Be gentle with yourself for the next few days because you will have used up a lot of emotional energy.

• *Monday 11 September* •

The more forward-thinking you are today, the better. It's a day for seeing the bigger picture without losing sight of those all-important details. You're ready to start a new chapter in your life, and you could receive some important news that will set you on the right track. Keep looking straight ahead and don't allow the past to pull you back.

• Tuesday 12 September •

You're so aware of your feelings today that it's difficult to be objective about anything because your emotions keep getting in the way. However, you do need to maintain some detachment if you're to make a balanced decision about a career move or a change of direction. A brainstorming session with a colleague or associate will give you a more rounded view of the situation and enable you to see how attainable your aspirations are.

• Wednesday 13 September •

Your code of ethics will be put to the test over the coming fortnight, and you will have to think seriously about how to respond to a certain proposition. As a matter of principle you prefer everything to be above board, but in this instance your emotions will sway your judgement and confuse the issue. As tempting as the offer seems, you may have to sort out some nagging doubts before you feel you can take it any further.

• Thursday 14 September •

There's a surprise in store for you today that will alter any arrangements you have already made. This suits you down to the ground and gives you the chance to discover a completely different side of yourself. If you thought you were somebody who needs at least 24 hours' notice in order to change your plans, you're about to find out just how flexible you can be. You'll see a new side to yourself!

• Friday 15 September •

Celebrate the fact that you're feeling like your old self again by being as sociable as possible today. You're in the mood for an intimate get-together with people that you always feel safe with and have a genuine affection for. This might end up costing you more than you bargained for, but you'll have a great time in the process. You'll also enjoy strolling around your favourite shops.

• Saturday 16 September •

There's a spanner in the works today and something you were hoping would happen gets delayed. Part of you wants to jump up and down with frustration or tear someone off a strip. However, you will soon feel better if you can work off these frustrated feelings by doing something physical. Any activity that you have to put your back into will give you the outlet you need for all that pent-up aggression.

• Sunday 17 September •

Listen to your hunches today because they'll be spot on. You can see through somebody's mask and discover what they're really thinking. It may surprise you to discover how accurate your intuition can be. Over the coming six weeks you'll have a lot more energy than usual, so put it to good use. It's the perfect time to launch a new venture, take the initiative in some way or rise to a challenge that would normally daunt you.

• Monday 18 September •

Eureka! Your thinking is so innovative and inventive today that you could come up with a brilliant scheme to change your working pattern without having to lose out financially. For a while you've been mulling over your various options on how to improve your existing situation, but until now nothing seemed workable. It just shows that things can change overnight!

• Tuesday 19 September •

If someone's got stars in their eyes and they're looking at you, there's only one conclusion you can reach. It may take you a few minutes to catch on because you had no idea that you had a secret admirer – least of all someone you see almost everyday. If you can't reciprocate their feelings, let them down gently because they're bound to be disappointed.

• Wednesday 20 September •

Think about your finances today, especially if you want to check that everything is running smoothly. You may have to write a letter to follow up an important transaction or you might want to double-check your last bank statement. It's also a good day for talking to a boss or superior about one of your ideas, especially if you are anxious to be given more responsibility or to prove yourself at work.

• Thursday 21 September •

A loved one needs your understanding today. Thank goodness they won't feel disappointed! Showing them how much you care through a thoughtful gesture or kind act will assuage their fears and give them the reassurance they need. Perhaps you could take them to their favourite restaurant or buy them a special treat that you know they'll be thrilled with. If you're broke, even a bar of chocolate will let them know you care.

• Friday 22 September •

Try not to saddle yourself with too many duties and responsibilities today or you'll end up feeling resentful at having so much on your plate. Your natural instinct may be to take on more than you can cope with, but before you say 'yes' to everything, consider whether it's really necessary to keep so busy. Either someone is taking advantage of you or you're expecting too much of yourself.

• Saturday 23 September •

If you've been working round the clock recently, you'll soon begin to see how much your efforts have paid off. Your social standing is highlighted and you'll start to move in ever wider circles as you gain more recognition for your talents. Although you may not be exactly pushy by nature, nevertheless, now is the time to start putting yourself forward.

• Sunday 24 September •

Trying to voice your needs and emotions will be a tall order today because you feel rather withdrawn, and you'll need to explain to a loved one why you're being so quiet and shy. They might have already got the wrong end of the stick and accused you of being unemotional, in which case all you can do is tell them how difficult it is to put your feelings into words at the moment.

• Monday 25 September •

Nothing ventured, nothing gained! If you have never considered alternative medicine before, this could be the ideal time to look into it. It may well do the trick and clear up an annoying symptom that has been dragging on and not responded to more conventional treatment. You will also benefit from reading about new ways of keeping fit and healthy, such as trying a different diet or taking extra vitamins.

• *Tuesday 26 September* •

You disappear into a world of your own today and, even though you are physically present, your mind is miles away. This would be a terrific day to go to a yoga class or to do some meditation, because it will exactly suit your mood. Anything that complements how you're feeling and enhances your well-being is good for you now. If your everyday reality impinges on your dreamy state, at least you'll be more relaxed to deal with it.

• *Wednesday 27 September* •

A love affair turns a corner today and you'll be looking at where you go from here. If you decide to make a commitment to this person, it's important that you don't gloss over any difficulties between you because they're not likely to go away of their own accord. Try to be as realistic as possible about how you feel about each other – especially the things that most irritate you.

• *Thursday 28 September* •

Be prepared to duck today because someone is in such a bad mood that they're liable to throw a wobbly. Keeping well out of their way is your safest bet, at least until they've calmed down enough to be coherent. This may have nothing – or everything – to do with you and sooner or later you'll have to get to the bottom of why they're so upset. In the meantime, it may be a wise move to keep your head down.

• *Friday 29 September* •

Talk about hot and steamy! There is a lot of unbridled passion between you and a certain someone today, so enjoy it while you get the chance. You might decide to go somewhere romantic for the weekend and make the most of your desire to be together – not that you'll take in much of the scenery! The priority is to have time away from all the stresses and strains of everyday life to enjoy the magic between you.

• Saturday 30 September •

The recent tension is starting to drain away and you've beginning to recharge your batteries. You feel an almost telepathic link with a certain person today and you can anticipate what they need without a word passing between you. They will also be able to tune into you. The wonderful moments of closeness that you share will be incredibly healing, both physically and emotionally.

OCTOBER AT A GLANCE

Love	♥ ♥
Money	£ $ £ $
Career	💻
Health	☼ ☼

• Sunday 1 October •

You're fired up with energy today and feeling on top of the world. In fact, you feel so benevolent and good-humoured that it's a joy to be with you. You're also in the mood to do some spending and you're ready to splash out on something special. Going to a lavish restaurant and having a slap-up meal would be a perfect end to a glorious weekend. Enjoy!

• Monday 2 October •

Do you feel as though you're being backed into a corner? If someone tries to impose their will on you today you'll have a job to say no to them. Precisely why they are being so forceful isn't clear, but you suspect that they have a hidden agenda. Rather than give in and let them walk all over you, try to use a little psychology on them to find out why they're so set on doing things their way.

• Tuesday 3 October •

Your finances receive a boost today and you'll hear some good news concerning an investment you made or a policy that you took out. If you've been careful with money in the past, you may begin to feel like being a little less cautious now and having some fun with it. You don't have to do anything very reckless or foolhardy, but you are in the mood to make the most of your resources.

• Wednesday 4 October •

Don't take anything or anyone for granted today because you could come unstuck. You should also avoid the temptation of taking any short cuts because you are bound to end up having to go back to square one and start again. You may have to enlist some help if you have got to tackle lots of outstanding jobs because, although they really need to be done, you're not remotely in the mood to work.

• Thursday 5 October •

Are you currently single? Well, you won't be for long if fate takes a hand in today's events! You could meet somebody socially who has a profound effect on you and it will be hard to think of anything or anyone else. The thrill of the chase isn't something that Virgos normally engage in, but you're so fascinated by this person that you might act out of character and do all the running. This could turn out to be a marathon, so pace yourself.

• *Friday 6 October* •

Everything seems to speed up today and you'll have to go up a gear to cope with the increased level of activity. If you're at work, it will be all hands on deck because there will be a frantic rush to get something finished on time. While everyone else has steam coming out of their ears, try to keep your cool and tell yourself that getting het up will only make matters worse. Maintaining your composure will help you to get things done.

• *Saturday 7 October* •

Do you feel like having a quiet, relaxing weekend? Forget it! A partner will keep changing their minds about what they want to do, which will make planning anything almost impossible. You're completely stumped as to why they're behaving so erratically, and every time you try to broach the subject you get an ear-bashing. If you get really fed up with this you may decide to do your own thing and leave them to it.

• *Sunday 8 October* •

If you feel that something is lacking in your life, then why not think about expanding your mental horizons and taking up a new area of study over the next few days. You may not want to commit yourself to a long-term course, but there are lots of other, more informal ways to learn. Simply getting a book out of the library can often be the first step on a voyage of discovery.

• *Monday 9 October* •

If you're beginning to question something that you've always thought to be true, it could be that you've reached a crossroads in your life and that you're beginning to look at things differently. Replacing an old belief that no longer holds water with a new and fresh perspective is a liberating experience,

and one that keeps you receptive to the idea of changing other outworn attitudes as well.

• *Tuesday 10 October* •

A loving relationship gives you the reassurance and support you need to make a difficult decision today. You might have lacked the courage to follow things through if it hadn't been for the fact that your strongest ally is backing you all the way. It's at times like these that you can count your blessings and appreciate the resources you have to draw on, both emotionally through other people and through your own strengths.

• *Wednesday 11 October* •

You can make progress today in an area where you feel you've been treading water for a while. Funds could be released so that you can get on with a project, or someone who has the say-so may finally give you the go-ahead on something. You will happily rise to the challenge of embarking on a new enterprise – so much so that you're likely to throw yourself into this to the exclusion of everything else. Perhaps you need to exercise a little moderation!

• *Thursday 12 October* •

Wow! Opportunity is about to knock on your door big time, so make sure the lights are on and someone's at home. Either you're going to be given a leg up the career ladder or a certain person will put in a good word for you and suddenly you will be flavour of the month. Enjoy the limelight and savour the fact that you now have everything to gain. Life is about to open up to you in some wonderful ways.

• *Friday 13 October* •

Today's Full Moon puts the accent on partnerships of all kinds, and if there are any skeletons in the cupboard, they're

likely to start to rattle over the coming two weeks. Don't be too
put off by today's date but concentrate instead on creating the
right climate for an honest discussion with someone. A set-to
is only likely if one of you is heaping all the blame on the other
and not wanting to face the truth. So be fair-minded and all
will be well.

• *Saturday 14 October* •

You're prepared to dig your heels in today if you can't get your
own way. It seems as if a certain person wants you to do things
in the tried and tested way, and you intuitively feel that a
more creative approach would work better. It could be a case of
an irresistible force meeting an immovable object – in other
words, there will be a big explosion when you both blow your
top. Someone will have to resolve the impasse.

• *Sunday 15 October* •

Jump at the chance to be sociable today because you could do
with having some fun. Yesterday's stubborn and bad-tem-
pered mood has been replaced by a more light-hearted state
of mind, and you don't want to waste any more time locking
horns with anyone. You could meet someone who has some
valuable contacts and is interested in working with you in
some way.

• *Monday 16 October* •

The more you put your heart and soul into everything you do
today, the more you'll see how grateful people are for the
input you give them and the level of commitment you have.
Everything has a knock-on effect, and the ripples that extend
from your contribution have more of an impact than you
realize. This may not be apparent at the moment but it soon
will be. It's food for thought, isn't it?

• *Tuesday 17 October* •

Expressing your feelings will be as easy as falling off a log today and you'll freely discuss even the most intimate details with other people, even if you don't know them very well. Granted, you do feel totally at home with them and would gladly tell them your life story given half the chance. Baring your soul in this way has a therapeutic effect on you and will encourage you to be honest about your emotions. It could be a very educational day.

• *Wednesday 18 October* •

If the atmosphere between you and a neighbour has been rather frosty recently, you now have the chance to break the ice and get back on speaking terms. You may have to swallow your pride and be the first one to offer the olive branch, but at least this proves that you have no desire to bear a grudge. Be prepared to do lots of talking and to charm them into being chummy once more.

• *Thursday 19 October* •

There's a strong emotional overtone to any decision you make today and this could have an important effect on your future. Give yourself plenty of time to mull over how you really feel because if you're acting out of anger or hurt, you may set off a chain reaction that does more harm than good. Wait until you're feeling less vulnerable before you take any important actions.

• *Friday 20 October* •

If you've been pushing the boat out recently where spending is concerned, you may need to tighten your belt for a while. If you sit down and work out exactly what your outgoings have been of late, you can then decide on a budget to see you through the coming weeks. Cutting down doesn't have to be any great hardship if you can view it as a means to an end.

• Saturday 21 October •

If you've got the day off, try to find time to attend to all things that need to be done around the house. You might feel really ambitious and decide to tackle some major chores, or you could compromise by doing some simple cleaning and tidying up. If you opt for the former, don't bite off more than you can chew in case you run out of steam halfway through. It might also help to rope in other family members.

• Sunday 22 October •

There is no doubt about your feelings for you-know-who today but you may not feel so sure that they are reciprocated. Is this true or are you imagining the worst? Your insecurity could mean that you read all sorts of stressful meanings into situations that are really quite harmless. Rather than spend hours agonizing over whether your fears are true or not, it will be much less exhausting to say what's in your heart and put yourself out of your misery.

• Monday 23 October •

It looks like being a difficult day where dealings with authority figures are concerned. Someone who calls the shots may be acting in a very high-handed way and testing your self-restraint to breaking point. You'll need to tread a fine line between showing that you're not easily intimidated, and making sure that you don't jeopardize everything you've worked so hard for.

• Tuesday 24 October •

There's so much gossip whirling around at the moment that it's hard to separate fact from fiction. Someone may be deliberately spreading a rumour and you would be wise not to believe anything you hear until you can get to the truth. Similarly, if you're having to negotiate with people who may not be as reliable as you would like, make sure you check out their credentials before committing yourself.

• Wednesday 25 October •

If you were to enter a popularity contest today, there is no doubt that you'd win first prize. Your charm and confidence are at an all-time high and your recent insecurities seem like a distant memory. Your new-found certainty about where you stand, in both your personal and professional life, comes as a huge relief. Dinner for two somewhere special would send your happiness sky high!

• Thursday 26 October •

You're seeing the world through rose-tinted spectacles today and everything certainly appears to be looking good. The accent continues to be on pleasure, enjoyment and spending as much time as possible with the people you love and care for. You will gain a tremendous amount of joy and comfort from being in familiar surroundings and, for the moment, you're content to stay on home ground.

• Friday 27 October •

Today's New Moon bodes well for any meetings, discussions or signing of agreements during the coming fortnight. Provided you've done your homework (and what Virgo wouldn't?) you will impress everyone by saying all the right things at the right time and bowling everyone over with your expertise and winning personality. Don't have a moment's doubt – you'll be absolutely fine.

● *Saturday 28 October* ●

You're in a soul-searching mood today and looking for more depth and substance to everything in your life. You're not content to stay on a superficial level – you want to find out what's going on beneath the surface. This means you can learn a lot about yourself and what makes you tick now, as well as gaining a better understanding of those closest to you. This will be invaluable.

● *Sunday 29 October* ●

If you're normally tentative about saying what you think, you'll surprise yourself by how forthright and direct you are today. In fact, if anything, you may have to make a conscious effort not to get too carried away and put someone's back up in the process. If something needs to be addressed, by all means confront the issue but stay in control and try not to delve into things that are none of your business.

● *Monday 30 October* ●

You could have a flash of inspiration today that leads to a mental journey of exploration. As a result, you might come up with some highly original insights that set you buzzing. It's almost as if you've just been zapped with 5,000 jolts of electricity – and you feel great! Take advantage of this powerful energy because it could revolutionize your life in some way.

● *Tuesday 31 October* ●

Are you ready to put your money where your mouth is? After yesterday's electrifying experience, you're all set to get to work and put your new-found ideas to the test. You need to find a way of integrating these exciting concepts into your life, otherwise they will simply be interesting theories that you talk about but never put into practice. Discuss them with a like-minded friend and get some feedback.

NOVEMBER AT A GLANCE

Love	♥ ♥ ♥ ♥
Money	£ $
Career	💻
Health	☼

• *Wednesday 1 November* •

Recent events have made you rethink your priorities and see them in a new light. The conclusions you come to may be a surprise to the people who expect you to stay the same forever, but not to those who know that life is all about change. It's not that you're about to throw the baby out with the bathwater – there are still many aspects of your life that are well worth conserving – but nevertheless you are thirsting for change.

• *Thursday 2 November* •

You continue to vibrate with energy and you're galvanized into action today by some good news that will make life more exciting. The everyday pattern of your life is changing and, although things haven't completely taken shape yet, you're beginning to get the picture. Nobody could accuse you of having been a stick-in-the-mud recently – you are far too forward-thinking for that!

• *Friday 3 November* •

Communications could go slightly haywire today, so be prepared for either a misunderstanding or for something to go missing. It might actually be you who's the culprit, because you've got your head in the clouds and you're not really paying attention to what's happening around you. Try to temper your day-dreaming with an occasional dose of reality. Even so, it's a fabulous day for letting your imagination run riot.

• *Saturday 4 November* •

Letting your mind wander off in all sorts of new directions has been a tremendous inspiration to you, but you may come up against some resistance today to the directions in which your new ideas are taking you. Could it be that a loved one feels that you're rocking the boat or is worried that you will soon get bored with your relationship? Give them the chance to air their views.

• *Sunday 5 November* •

Be careful not to jump to any hasty conclusions if yesterday's discussion has left you feeling disheartened and wondering where you go from here. It's much more likely to be teething problems than irreconcilable differences, but you still have a long way to go before you can both see eye to eye. A healthy relationship can allow for differences of opinion, provided you can respect each other.

• *Monday 6 November* •

You need lots of company today because you'll feel suffocated if you spend too much time alone. You're in an extremely talkative mood and the more you can get off your chest the better. You could make some very useful contacts to help further your career in some way, and someone may make it very plain that they're interested in your talents. It's a great day for attending a job interview or important meeting.

• *Tuesday 7 November* •

Are you playing fast and loose with someone or is it the other way round? If you're the one who is playing with someone's heart, it could be a sign that you want more freedom and are feeling emotionally hemmed in. It's not that you don't take your commitments seriously, it's simply that you need a little more room for manoeuvre from a partner. That doesn't mean to say, however, that you're no longer accountable for what you do.

• *Wednesday 8 November* •

Do you still want to strike a blow for freedom? Your rebellious mood expresses itself in a different way today and a bone of contention between you and a colleague or boss could escalate into all-out war. Before you go completely OTT, think about the likely consequences of sparking off a heated debate. Unless you truly don't care what happens, try to temper your words with a little Virgo caution.

• *Thursday 9 November* •

You don't have to worry about minding your Ps and Qs today because you're in a much more conciliatory mood than you were yesterday. Concentrate on restoring a more amicable atmosphere and, if apologies are in order, don't allow any false pride to get in the way. Getting on your high horse is all well and good, but you must also be prepared to climb down again if absolutely necessary.

• *Friday 10 November* •

A fun-loving mood starts to steal over you today, giving you a fabulous excuse to have a get-together with some good friends. The ball's in your court, so why not get out your address book and start ringing round and seeing who's free. Rather than limit yourself to the people who you see regularly, why not call some chums you really like but rarely see.

• *Saturday 11 November* •

If you already have plenty of social activities lined up for this weekend, be prepared for a few more unexpected invitations to come along now, just to make life more interesting. You'd rather be spoilt for choice than sit around twiddling your thumbs, but the downside is that you may end up upsetting someone by having to turn them down. That's the price of popularity. . . .

• Sunday 12 November •

There are so many comings and goings today that you'll probably crave a little peace and quiet before too long. If you feel as though you're spending the whole day chasing after people and firming up arrangements, you could be tempted to let them all get on with it, and spend the rest of the time with one or two of your nearest and dearest.

• Monday 13 November •

Feel like enjoying the high life? Well, you can today because there's something to celebrate and you'll do it in style. A boss or client could be so pleased with your performance that they want to show their appreciation by taking you out or giving you a treat. Your love life will bring you plenty of joy and happiness over the next few weeks, so you've got lots to look forward to. It's perfect for enjoying a glorious festive season.

• Tuesday 14 November •

Be very careful that you don't misread a situation today and end up in an embarrassing position. If you thought you had the measure of someone, they might send out some very strange signals now which are hard to interpret. They may be deliberately leading you up the garden path, in which case you need to treat them with extreme suspicion. Forewarned is forearmed.

• *Wednesday 15 November* •

It's time to shake off the cobwebs! Jovial and light-hearted is the best way to describe your mood today. Life seems full of excitement and you feel like doing something on the spur of the moment. Ideally, you should give your usual routine a miss but if that isn't possible, at least think of something different to do at some point today. Acting on impulse will give you a real buzz.

• *Thursday 16 November* •

The planetary spotlight is shining on your area of relationships today and highlighting some ambivalence in your feelings for someone. If you still haven't resolved the conflict between your burning desire for intimacy and your need to maintain your own independence, you could find a way forward now. Maybe you need to discover that the two things are not necessarily mutually exclusive.

• *Friday 17 November* •

If someone is being a bit of a prima donna today, your best bet is to pay as little attention to them as possible and let them get on with it. Ignoring them will hopefully have the desired effect and they'll calm down. If they persist with their amateur dramatics in the hope of getting you to rise to the bait, they're in for a big disappointment. You've got more important things to do!

• *Saturday 18 November* •

What's got into a certain person? If you can't bear the thought of tiptoeing around them on eggshells for a minute longer, it's time to make your feelings known. Explain to them how their mood is affecting you, and try to find out what's bugging them so much. A little tender loving care may help them to open up and finally disclose the reason for their petulant behaviour.

• *Sunday 19 November* •

You may have been through the mill on the emotional front recently but you can take heart today because there's a positive shift to calmer waters. You're able to discuss some very delicate issues with a loved one without getting caught up in a lot of emotion or recrimination. At last you can gain some form of emotional perspective and find a way forward.

• *Monday 20 November* •

If you feel like buying a gift for someone, this is the day to go shopping. If you know their taste inside out, you won't have any trouble finding exactly the right thing. It could be a little trickier if you haven't got a lot of clues or if this person is difficult to buy for. Rather than err on the side of caution, follow your intuition, even if you spot something that seems an unlikely choice.

• *Tuesday 21 November* •

It's a fabulous day to contemplate your finances and work out new ways to make your money grow. Investing any spare cash you might have will pay dividends later, and it'll be reassuring to know that you've got a nest-egg for the future, no matter how small it is. It could pay to get expert advice before you go ahead because you might as well get the best returns you possibly can.

• *Wednesday 22 November* •

You'll be able to get a great deal done today, especially if you give yourself wholeheartedly to whatever it is you're doing. Your physical reserves are so great that you can push yourself to the limit and still not feel depleted. If you feel passionate about your work, your motivation will be tenfold and you'll be able to keep going for as long as you need to. Once that's over, relax and give yourself a well-deserved breather!

• *Thursday 23 November* •

Your enthusiasm alone will inspire colleagues to work with more dedication than usual. You're a shining example to them at the moment and your dynamic approach is getting every-one moving. If you've never contemplated being in a leader-ship position, you can now get a taste of what it's like to motivate a team. You might decide that you like this and you want more of it in the future!

• *Friday 24 November* •

Talk about emotional blackmail! You'll be completely taken aback today by someone's blatant and underhand tactics. You don't know whether you're more shocked by their dishonesty or the fact that you would never have suspected that they were capable of such behaviour. Even though you're clear about not letting yourself be manipulated, you aren't so convinced about the future of the relationship.

• *Saturday 25 November* •

If you're concerned about a medical problem, get it sorted now or you'll go on procrastinating forever. Whatever the symp-toms are, they're probably brought on by stress, but don't worry because there are all sorts of self-help techniques that you can learn in order to manage it better. Once you've had yourself checked out, look into ways of countering the effects of your busy lifestyle.

• *Sunday 26 November* •

You may be more concerned with somebody else's welfare than your own today, and will want to spend time helping them in some way. Perhaps they've been unwell and they need some practical support, or they may simply need a sympathetic ear. Virgos often take it upon themselves to serve others in some way and, true to type, you're more than happy to give of yourself now.

• *Monday 27 November* •

Keep a notebook to hand today and write down any thoughts and ideas that pop into your head. They may not seem that mind-blowing at the time but at some future date they may prove to be very significant indeed. You should also keep an open channel of communication between you and a colleague or partner, just in case you have a brainwave that you'd dismiss otherwise.

• *Tuesday 28 November* •

If you want to capitalize on your extraordinarily buoyant mood today, reach out to as many people as possible in an effort to promote yourself and your talents. Knocking on doors can often be a dispiriting exercise, but with such a strong belief in yourself even a lukewarm reception will be like water off a duck's back. Go for gold and don't settle for less!

• *Wednesday 29 November* •

Today's planetary line-up is very supportive of your attempts to prove yourself to the world and you can take comfort in the knowledge that you're doing the right thing. Finding your niche hasn't been a piece of cake, but now that you know what you want, there's nothing stopping you from getting it.

Not only that, but you've also got all the back-up you need. The world is your oyster!

• *Thursday 30 November* •

Your sense of duty and responsibility comes to the fore today and you consider it very important to honour any commitments you have. A loved one may remind you of a promise that you made, and you will do everything in your power to keep it. Knowing that you're a person who keeps their word gives you a sense of integrity and, above all, self-respect.

DECEMBER AT A GLANCE

Love	❤ ❤ ❤ ❤ ❤
Money	£ $
Career	💻 💻 💻 💻 💻
Health	☼ ☼ ☼ ☼ ☼

• *Friday 1 December* •

As the end of the year approaches, you're looking forward to the future and thinking about any aspects of your life that belong firmly in the past. These may be outworn attitudes or habits – or even people – that you've let go of to make room for the new. Don't be in a rush to fill the empty spaces because things will slot into place in their own good time.

• *Saturday 2 December* •

How are you getting on with your Christmas shopping? If you haven't even started yet, this is an ideal day to get going and check out what's on offer in the shops. In your own inimitable way, you've probably already compiled a list and decided which presents you want to buy. You may even have com-

pleted half your shopping already. It will take you no time at
all to whizz round today and find exactly what you're looking
for.

• Sunday 3 December •

Feeling hot under the collar? You're in rather an impatient
mood today and easily irritated if you have to wait around for
anyone. As a result you may overreact and make a big deal out
of nothing. If you feel yourself boiling over with frustration,
rather than find a scapegoat for your bad mood, try to work it
off doing something physical. Or how about trying those anti-
stress techniques you've been investigating recently?

• Monday 4 December •

A certain person is keeping you in check today, and woe betide
if you step out of line. Why do they feel such a need to control
you? Whatever their motives, you'll feel suffocated by them
and desperate for a let-out clause. You'll need to decide if this
particular relationship has had its day or whether you need to
make a stand, because you no longer wish to put up with such
behaviour.

• Tuesday 5 December •

If you've been given the job of getting everyone together for a
festive outing, strike while the iron is hot and start making the
arrangements today. If you've all decided that you don't want
to stint and you'd love to go somewhere special, pull out all
the stops and choose a place that's really classy. Where else
can you dress up to the nines and be treated like royalty?

• Wednesday 6 December •

You're certainly in a festive mood today, and the more you can
party between now and Christmas the better. Fortunately, you

can afford to coast along at work at the moment and so you can devote yourself wholeheartedly to unadulterated pleasure. If you're currently single and looking for romance, the coming weeks could offer a source of rich pickings!

• *Thursday 7 December* •

It's one of those days when it's impossible to stick to a routine or get down to anything because something unexpected keeps happening. Not that you're complaining because you'll welcome any distraction from work at the moment. You've got a million things on your mind that have nothing to do with what you should be focusing on, and everything to do with you-know-who.

• *Friday 8 December* •

You're prone to being gullible today and someone could, consciously or unconsciously, exploit that. Don't say yes to anyone who doesn't have a proven track record, especially if it seems as if butter wouldn't melt in their mouth. They may be too good to be true. Even someone who's normally trustworthy and reliable could let you down now. Compensate for any disappointments by doing something you love.

• *Saturday 9 December* •

Talk about bees to the honeypot! Get ready for heads to turn because you feel absolutely at your best today. With luck, your social diary is jam-packed with invitations to go out this weekend, because you don't intend to spend a single moment at home. Your powers of attraction are at an all-time high – so much so that you won't be safe unless you hire a bodyguard!

• *Sunday 10 December* •

You're in love with love today and your heart is bursting with joy. You've been swept off your feet by some intoxicating feelings and you're not nearly ready to come back down to earth. In fact, you'd be happy to stay floating on cloud nine ad infinitum, and although that may be a tall order, you intend to make the most of the time you spend there.

• *Monday 11 December* •

Somebody you know well, either personally or professionally, will test your patience over the coming fortnight. They are being very inflexible and they may also have very strong ideas about what is right and what's wrong. Although it will take a lot to get your back up now, you still won't condone their behaviour and you'll feel that it's your duty to challenge them. Watch their reaction, because this is something they don't expect from you.

• *Tuesday 12 December* •

If you have guests staying over the holiday period, now is the time to start getting the house ready for their visit. Organizing as much as you can in advance will minimize the pre-festive panic and allow you more time for those last-minute shopping trips. This is a good opportunity to have a turn out and to throw away any bits and pieces that you no longer need.

• *Wednesday 13 December* •

Ooops! You may have spent more than you intended to over the last few days and you'll be furiously trying to balance the books today to see what's left over. Extravagance is your middle name at the moment and you want to extend your generosity of spirit to as many people as possible. Oh well, Christmas does come only once a year after all. Just as well, by the looks of it!

• Thursday 14 December •

You're in one of those sensitive states in which you're susceptible to the moods of the people around you. That's all well and good if you happen to feel comfortable with them, but if there's anyone in your orbit who's in the habit of riding roughshod over your feelings, you should do your best to avoid them today. Come to think of it, what are they doing in your life anyway?

• Friday 15 December •

If anyone you know is down in the mouth today, you'll soon do your best to cheer them up. Your good mood is obvious to everyone and it's highly infectious to boot, so before too long you'll have shaken them out of the doldrums. The pace of life is picking up and you can feel yourself going up a gear just to keep up with the increased momentum. Let yourself get swept along in the social current and you'll be fine.

• Saturday 16 December •

If you're going out of town today you'll have the most wonderful time. You'll be amongst your favourite people in a delightfully festive ambience, and the only thing you'll have to watch is your tendency to overindulge. That's not to say you shouldn't enjoy yourself to the hilt, it just depends on how fragile you'll want to feel tomorrow morning.

• Sunday 17 December •

You could have a big battle with yourself today over whether to make any last-minute purchases. The devil-may-care side of you doesn't want to be restrained by financial considerations, but your practical side is already having kittens at the idea of overspending. If you do decide to throw caution to the winds and venture off to the shops, remember that it's the thought that counts and not how much money you spend.

• Monday 18 December •

If you're still a lone Virgo and you haven't managed to be snatched up yet, make sure that you're out and about today because there's still time to meet that special someone. You've been radiating a certain *je ne sais quoi* for some time now, so be prepared to work your magic on whoever you decide to captivate. Keep your eyes peeled for someone special!

• Tuesday 19 December •

You might be feeling slightly on edge today, so before you get completely snowed under you should enlist someone's help. There's no reason to do everything on your own, unless you believe that you can do things better than anyone else. It may be true that not everyone is as careful as you are to get everything just so, but not everyone happens to be a perfectionist! Maybe you should relax and learn to delegate.

• Wednesday 20 December •

You're so busy with the forthcoming festivities that you've hardly got a moment to yourself today. Far from being exhausted by it all, you'll feel positively energized and love every minute of it. If you were thinking about stocking up the freezer ready for the holidays, why not capitalize on your boundless energy and get some of the cooking out of the way today. It'll cut down the amount of work to do later on, and give you more time to let your hair down.

• Thursday 21 December •

Who's in the dog house? The pre-Christmas tension seems to have got to a certain person and it looks as if it will be your job to smooth some ruffled feathers. The last thing you want to have to deal with is an emotional outburst, but at least that's preferable to allowing a bad mood to spoil everything. You can't help but show your disappointment, and you'll make it quite clear that you don't want it to happen again.

• *Friday 22 December* •

Why not spoil yourself and have a lovely treatment at a top beauty salon? You deserve to look your best, and with all the admiring glances you're receiving at the moment, you might as well give them their money's worth! And while you're spending your hard-earned cash on enhancing your looks, why not complete the image by getting that stunning outfit you've had your eye on?

• *Saturday 23 December* •

It's a day for rolling up your sleeves and ploughing through the list of things to do. If all hands are on deck, you'll accomplish miracles in next to no time, not to mention having fun in the process. It may be sheer elbow grease that gets the job done, but it's a wonderfully satisfying feeling to give something your best shot.

• *Sunday 24 December* •

There's a lot of sexual tension in the air today and it could be that one of you is playing hard to get. You probably won't be able to keep it up for long, and the odds are that you'll end up succumbing to each other's irresistible charms. With all the preparations done and most of the presents wrapped, it looks as though you can enjoy a romantic Christmas Eve.

• *Monday 25 December* •

Happy Christmas! It promises to be a very enjoyable day with everyone delighted to be together. There's a lot of good humour and wit in the air and you'll be in the mood for fun and games, especially group ones like charades. Nobody will feel in the least inhibited, whether that means showing affection or being willing to make fools of yourselves.

• *Tuesday 26 December* •

Your emotions go very deep today and you have a powerful sense of how much you love your nearest and dearest. You're also moved by how kind and generous everyone has been and how thoughtfully your presents were chosen. You may even shed a tear or two, especially if you happen to be watching something sentimental on television.

• *Wednesday 27 December* •

If you feel as if you've been cooped up for too long, try to get out in the fresh air today and have a long walk. While other people are still recovering from various excesses, you're feeling surprisingly fresh and energetic, and the longer you stay out and exercise the better you'll feel. You might even steal a few peaceful moments to yourself.

• *Thursday 28 December* •

If you're thinking of putting your feet up for a rest, don't! Just when one lot of visitors are getting ready to leave, somebody else could show up on your doorstep completely out of the blue. An unannounced visit from this person is probably totally in character, and you'll no doubt be thrilled to see them. That, however, doesn't necessarily go for the rest of the family.

• *Friday 29 December* •

Elbows at the ready? You'll need them if the sales are beckoning and you have an irresistible urge to spend some money. Oh well, you might as well give in and see it as beneficial retail therapy. You may not be able to justify it that way to anybody else, but provided you don't go OTT, you should find some terrific bargains that everyone approves of. Happy hunting!

• *Saturday 30 December* •

This is a great day to make plans and think about any New Year resolutions that you might want to make. If you take your time and give your ideas some serious thought, you could come to the conclusion that there are a few important changes that you want to make in 2001. Keep these to yourself until you've decided how best to put them across.

• *Sunday 31 December* •

Are you all geared up to greet the New Year? You're definitely in the mood to enjoy yourself, and the more friends and loved ones you can be with, the more fun you'll have. Whether it's an intimate gathering or a noisy crowded party, you will be in your element and will quite happily mix with anyone and everyone. It looks as though you'll be shouting 'Happy New Year' the loudest!